Mindful Teaching Practices for Black Male Achievement

Mindful Teaching Practices for Black Male Achievement

A Student-Focused Guide for Educators

Theodore S. Ransaw

ROWMAN & LITTLEFIELD
Lanham • Boulder • New York • London

Published by Rowman & Littlefield
An imprint of The Rowman & Littlefield Publishing Group, Inc.
4501 Forbes Boulevard, Suite 200, Lanham, Maryland 20706
www.rowman.com

86-90 Paul Street, London EC2A 4NE, United Kingdom

British Library Cataloguing in Publication Information Available

Library of Congress Cataloging-in-Publication Data

Names: Ransaw, Theodore S., author.
Title: Mindful teaching practices for Black male achievement : a student-focused guide
   for educators / Theodore S. Ransaw.
Description: Lanham, Maryland : Rowman & Littlefield, 2022. | Includes bibliographical
   references and index. | Summary: "This book helps teachers think through strategies
   for building relationships, making connections, and creating 'aha' moments with
   Black males"—Provided by publisher.
Identifiers: LCCN 2022015828 (print) | LCCN 2022015829 (ebook) | ISBN
   9781475867336 (cloth) | ISBN 9781475867343 (paperback) | ISBN
   9781475867350 (epub)
Subjects: LCSH: African American boys—Education. | African American young men—
   Education. | Educational equalization—United States. | Academic achievement—
   Social aspects—United States.
Classification: LCC LC2717 .R26 2022 (print) | LCC LC2717 (ebook) | DDC
   371.829/96073—dc23/eng/20220623
LC record available at https://lccn.loc.gov/2022015828
LC ebook record available at https://lccn.loc.gov/2022015829

Contents

Foreword

Growing up as an African American male in Philadelphia, Pennsylvania's Logan section, where since the 1970s acute poverty, deferred dreams, and a systemic lack of resources for a dominant community of color were common occurrences, I learned over time that when someone believes in you, it provides the necessary fuel to propel you forward in life. Moreover, having the influential leadership of educators who took the responsibility of creating conditions for underserved children of color to learn, aspire, grow, and succeed is the added most necessary component to opening pathways of infinite possibilities for success in the K–12 school system and beyond in life.

Now as an educator for over twenty-five years and recognized as a highly effective superintendent of K–12 schools, through experiences, I remain cognizant of the historical constructs of African American males growing up in poverty and the ways in which influential mentorship has become one of the major pillars of success. Great teachers and influential leaders who understand poverty, the perceptual plights of young Black boys, and who build sustainable relationships with students play a major role in leading these children toward infinite possibilities of success.

Defeating poverty is a form of social justice in an ever-changing society, and those who motivate children of color—Black boys—to defeat the odds in beating poverty are in fact reframing the way students view their chances at success.

Dr. Theodore Ransaw not only understands the importance of the aforementioned, but he has also taken the courageous leap in examining the achievement of Black boys—gaps, deficiencies, and successes—while speaking truth to the issues that are systemic in nature. Moreover, Dr. Ransaw takes a deeper dive in the Black male experience in schools, while speaking to the core of educators by providing vivid experiences of current life occurrences, where Black males feel "the system" is against them, allowing no flexibility, compassion, or support to become successful.

In *Mindful Teaching Practices for Black Male Achievement*, Dr. Ransaw focuses deeply on how educators must balance academic and social capital in the classroom to motivate young Black men. For example, as recognized in any competitive sport, the athlete must understand the opponent through meticulous assessment, create a plan, implement the plan with fidelity, and evaluate the results on an ongoing basis for the next competition. In the afore-mentioned, Black males are in the fight of their life. The plan is focused on defying the odds. Implementation is navigating the "tight rope" of life involving the complexities and confluences of perception, manhood, violence, and institutionalized racism. The evaluation is learning from the ebbs and flows of the experiences—successes and needs for improvement.

Most important, Dr. Ransaw speaks the truth to the Black male experience. It's graphic, touching, emotional, and realistic. The famous musician Gil Scott Heron spoke with authenticity to African Americans struggling in America by stating in verse, "the revolution will not be televised," and Dr. Ransaw explicitly gives examples of how the revolution of Black males is now televised—trials, tribulations, unrest, arrest, murder, failures, and successes are on full display.

This information is fuel for influential educators, as we must know the past to understand the grand possibilities of the future. Educators cannot teach what they don't know and lead where they are afraid to go. Hence, Dr. Ransaw's *Mindful Teaching Practices for Black Male Achievement* provides educators with the historical constructs, current examples, and tools to encourage understanding to equip educators with the necessary tools to lead with authenticity—a thorough understanding and clear focus of the battlefield of life for African American boys. This is a must read for all educators, as information is power. It provides the information to motivate educators to lead unapologetically with doggish goals to reach Black boys and lead to infinite possibilities of success.

Khalid N. Mumin, EdD, 2021 Pennsylvania Superintendent of the Year, Superintendent, Lower Merion School District, Ardmore, Pennsylvania

Introduction

THE NEED FOR EQUALITY AND EQUITY

Blessed are the children . . . oh Lord, bless the children. Deliverance from the fruits of evil—you need devotion.

—"Devotion," Earth, Wind and Fire (1974)

The purpose of *Mindful Teaching Practices for Black Male Achievement* is to facilitate critical discussion of policies, attitudes toward, and outcomes regarding Black males and their experiences in education. It is intended to help parents, educators, organizations, and policy makers better understand the complex nature surrounding Black males (males of African and African American descent) to identify strategies for effecting positive change. Each of the chapters is fully referenced for those who would like additional information. The reader will also find reflection questions, prolepsis goal-setting questions, and vignettes at the end of each chapter, as well as a toolkit resource guide in the Appendix. While there have been significant advances toward equality as well as equity for Black males, more work obviously needs to be done. For example, all men may be equal under the law, but White and Black men do not get equitable justice or an equitable education in America. While the Emancipation Proclamation eliminated physical slavery in the United States, not all of America's people have quality choices that lead to a better life. The reality of Black males in this country is that too many of them face frequent barriers, negative perceptions, and low expectations for achievement in their daily lives from historic discrimination. This book provides resources for informed discussion surrounding the nuanced and complex nature of Black males.

WHY WRITE MINDFUL TEACHING PRACTICES
FOR BLACK MALE ACHIEVEMENT?

The American education system has not created a positive schooling experience for most Black males. Black male students suffer the most from school inequities. For example, Black males are more likely to be suspended and expelled from school, more likely to be placed in special education, less likely to graduate from high school, and less likely to enroll in college. On the other hand, Black women earn postsecondary degrees at higher rates than White women, Latinas, and Asians, while Black male college graduation rates are only at 35 percent (Bridge Builder, 2020). As American schools across the country are pressing reset after COVID-19, the time is right for a friendly, easy-to-use resource to support positive educational outcomes for Black males.

Supporting Black males benefits our overall society in many ways including the promotion of a healthy economy. When Black males are seen as having potential instead of being perceived as negative perceptions, people see the good in them and recognize the benefits they can achieve. Believing in Black males can foster the creation of a more inclusive workforce and facilitate intellectual choices that advance the human condition. For example, when young Black men graduate from high school, they help stabilize and build their communities and later become good fathers and good role models for other young Black men (Bligh, 2013). *Mindful Teaching Practices for Black Male Achievement* intends to supply stakeholders interested in improving the lives of Black males with such motivation.

BACKGROUND OF BLACK MALE INITIATIVES

At this reading, it seems as if there are more programs, conferences, symposiums, panels, and initiatives as well as policies about education for African Americans in general as well as Black males than ever before. We have the social media–driven movement Black Lives Matter, the White House's My Brother's Keeper Initiative, the Educational Excellence for African Americans Initiative, the Annual Black Male Development Symposium, the African American Boys Conference, the CUNY Annual Male Initiative, the Annual African American Male Youth Conference, the Campaign for Black Male Achievement, 100 Black Men of America, and the National Conference on Educating Black Children that has been in operation for twenty-eight years, to name just a few. However, while new research and critical discourse about Black males has become more popular in recent years, the work surrounding the unique circumstances Black males face in America has been going on for much longer (Murphy, 2010). For example, while not specifically about Black males, Carter G. Woodson wrote about the negative effects of the American education system for African Americans in his book *The Mis-Education of the Negro* way back in 1933. Contemporary authors have elaborated on this premise. For example, Dr. Jawanza Kunjufu (2004) has stated that to him, it seems as if there has been a conspiracy to destroy Black boys for more thanr thirty years.

In 1955, fourteen-year-old Emmitt Till was beaten and then murdered in Money, Mississippi, for allegedly whistling at a White female (Whitfield, 1991). That incident was one of the most egregious incidents in American history. But even fairly recently the murder of Black males is still rampant.

On August 9, 2014, twenty-eight-year-old White police officer Darren Wilson killed eighteen-year-old African American Michael Brown in Ferguson, Missouri. Michael Brown was unarmed, shot six times, and left on the street after the shooting for four hours. Officer Wilson later testified that Michael Brown had reached for his weapon, but eyewitnesses reported that Brown was not resisting and had his hands up in a "don't shoot" position. An autopsy by medical examiner Dr. Michael Baden determined that an analysis of the gunshot wounds supports claims that Michael Brown was not the aggressor (Chandler, 2014). Protests in Ferguson started almost immediately. The protests became so intense, not just in the United States but around the world, that Attorney General Eric Holder visited Ferguson personally. Holder's Ferguson report concluded that Blacks in Ferguson, Missouri, were discriminated against in a strategic manner. The US Department of Justice launched a civil rights investigation soon after.

A large part of the uproar about Michael Brown's shooting was fueled by the fact that it was not an isolated event. On April 21, 2015, Freddie Gray was arrested in Baltimore and died three days later from three broken vertebrae he received while in police custody. On July 17, 2014—one month before the Michael Brown shooting—Eric Garner was also killed by police officers in Staten Island, New York. Numerous highly publicized killings of other Black males by policemen have occurred over the past decade in the United States—namely, Timothy Stansbury—January 24, 2004, in Brooklyn, New York; Sean Bell—November 25, 2006, in Queens, New York; Oscar Grant—January 1, 2009, in Oakland, California; Aaron Campbell—January 29, 2010, in Portland, Oregon; Alonzo Ashley—July 18, 2011, in Denver, California; Wendell Allen—March 7, 2012, in New Orleans, Louisiana; Milton Hall—August 17, 2012, in Saginaw, Michigan; John Crawford—August, 2, 2013, in Beavercreek, Ohio; Ezell Ford—August 11, 2013, in Los Angeles, California; Dante Parker—Victorville, California; Jonathan Ferrell—September 16, 2013, in Charlotte, North Carolina; Tamir Rice—November 22, 2014, in

Cleveland, Ohio; Laquan McDonald—October 20, 2015, in Chicago, Illinois; Delrawn Small—July 4, 2016, in Brooklyn, New York; Alton Sterling—July, 6, 2016, in Baton Rouge, Louisiana; and Philando Castile—July 6, 2016, in Falcon Heights, Minnesota (Harkinson, 2013; Harris-Perry, 2014; Fantz, Almasy, & Shoichet, 2015). The majority of the shootings were largely publicized, influencing perceptions about how police officers view African American males. Tamir Rice's (a twelve year old who was killed while holding a toy gun) shooting was called "justifiable," Freddie Gray's case was ruled a mistrial, Eric Garner's shooter was not prosecuted, and Michael Brown's shooter was not indicted.

The killing of George Floyd on May 20, 2020, by Minneapolis police officer Derek Chauvin was another trial that has exposed what has been lingering in the shadows of America for far too long: police-enforced racism. George Floyd was an African American. Derek Chauvin is a White police officer. Chauvin held his knee on Floyd's neck while he was handcuffed on the ground for more than eight minutes. Floyd pleaded, "Please, man, I can't breathe," until he died. There were also three other police officers near Floyd, but they chose to not take a single action to save his life. Chauvin was charged with second-degree murder, and each of the other three officers were charged with one count of aiding and abetting second-degree murder and aiding and abetting second-degree manslaughter. On April 20, 2021, Chauvin was found guilty of murdering George Floyd. On June 23, Chauvin was sentenced to twenty-two and a half years in prison. The other three police officers involved, Thomas Lane, J. A. Kueng, and Tou Thao, were found guilty of all counts of violating George Floyd's civil rights at their federal trial and have pleaded not guilty to aiding and abetting second-degree murder and aiding and abetting second-degree manslaughter of Floyd's death (Jones, 2022).

Because George Floyd's murder was recorded and shared through social media, more than seventy million people, not just in the United States, but around the world, watched the murder in real time. The murder of George Floyd took place shortly after a series of recent killings of other African Americans. Ahmaud Arbery was shot and killed on February 23, 2020, in Glynn County, Georgia, while jogging. Breonna Taylor was shot and killed by police in Louisville, Kentucky, on March 13, 2020, in her apartment, while she was sleeping. These shootings and murders of Black people are similar to Philando Castile, Freddie Gray, Michael Brown, Eric Garner, Trayvon Martin, Amadou Diallo, Abner Louima, Malice Wayne Green, James Meredith, and Emmett Till.

Shockingly, during the George Floyd trial and within ten miles of the courthouse, Daunte Wright, an African American male, was shot to death after being stopped by a White female Minneapolis police officer Kim Potter for a traffic violation on April 11, 2021.

Other Black people killed by police in 2021 were: Carl Dorsey III, 39, Newark, New Jersey; La Garion Smith, 27, Homestead, Florida; Tre-Kedrian Tyquan White, 20, Richburg, South Carolina; Vincent Belmonte, 18, Cleveland, Ohio; Shawn McCoy, Spokane, Washington; Robert "Lil Rob" Howard, 30, Memphis, Tennessee; Kwamena Ocran, 24, Gaithersburg, Maryland; Jason Nightengale, 32, Evanston, Illinois; Matthew Oxendine, 46, Pembroke, North Carolina; Paul Bolden, 37, Phoenix, Arizona; Patrick Warren Sr., 52, Killeen, Texas; Lymond Maurice Moses, 30, Wilmington, Delaware; Kershawn Geiger, 24, Carmichael, California; Reginald Johnson, 48, Biloxi, Mississippi; Zonterious Johnson, 24, Lawton, Oklahoma; Christopher Harris, 27, Toledo, Ohio; Eusi Malik Kater Jr., 21, Titusville, Alabama; Tyree Kajawn Rogers, 38, Wichita Falls, Texas; Randy Miller, 55, Los Angeles, California; Roger D. Hipskind, 37, Wabash, Indiana; Karl Walker, 29, Dixon, California; Marvon Payton Jr., 27, Las Vegas, Nevada; Jenoah Donald, 30, Hazell Dell, Washington; Dontae Green, 34, Baltimore, Maryland; Trey Webster, 18, Mobile, Alabama; Christopher Hagans, 36, Stratford, Connecticut; Andrew Hogan, 25, Trotwood, Ohio; Dustin Demaurean Powell, 34, Lakeview, Texas; Gregory Taylor, 45, Seattle, Washington; Jordan Walton, 21, Austin, Texas; Cortez Lee Bogan, 27, East Cleveland, Ohio; Brandon Wimberly, 36, Coral Gables, Florida; De'Aire Jontae Gray, 28, Speedway, Indiana; Daverion Kinard, 29, Fontana, California; Arnell States, 39, Cedar Rapids, Iowa; Alonte Damar Murphy, 22, Garden City, Michigan; Benjamin Tyson, 35, Baltimore, Maryland; Donald Francis Hairston, 44, Culpeper, Virginia; Chandra Moore, 55, Detroit, Michigan; Broderick Woods, 33, Houston, Texas; Dwight Brown, 41, Abbeville, Louisiana; Andrew Teague, 43, Columbus, Ohio; Howayne Gayle, 35, Lakeland, Florida; Tyshon Jones, 29, Rochester, New York; Tyrell Wilson, 32, Danville, California; Nika Nicole Holbert, 31, Nashville, Tennessee; Charles Ray Phillips, 51, Monahans, Texas; Christopher Ruffin, 28, Palm Bay, Florida; Caleb Smith, 22, Hayward, California; Matthew James Hurlock, 35, Cypress, Texas; Exzabian Morgan Myers, 31, Graniteville, South Carolina; Daryl Leonard Jordan, 50, Miami, Florida; Kevin L. Duncan, 38, Bellefontaine, Ohio; Frankie Jennings, 32, Charlotte, North Carolina; Aaron Pierre Thomas, Canton, Ohio; Travon Chadwell, 18, Chicago, Illinois; Malcolm D. Johnson, 31, Kansas City, Missouri; Donovon W. Lynch, 25, Virginia Beach, Virginia; Matthew Blaylock, 38, Los Angeles, California; Michael Leon Hughes, 32, Jacksonville, Florida; Willie Roy Allen, 57, Lithonia, Georgia; DeShawn Latiwon Tatum, 25, Rock Island, Illinois; Noah R. Green, 25, Washington, DC; Diwone Wallace, 24, Alorton, Illinois; Gabriel Casso, 21, Bronx, New York; Desmon Montez Ray, 28, Birmingham, Alabama; Roger Cornelius Allen, 44, Daly City, California; Dominique Williams, 32, Takoma Park, Maryland; James Lionel Johnson, 38, Takoma

Park, Maryland; James Alexander, 24, Philadelphia, Pennsylvania; Raheem Reeder, 21, Tallahassee, Florida; Deshund Tanner, 31, Georgetown, Kentucky; Faustin Guetigo, 27, Rockford, Illinois; Daunte Wright, 20, Brooklyn Center, Minnesota; Miles Jackson, 27, Westerville, Ohio; Matthew Zadok Williams, 35, Decatur, Georgia; Anthony Thompson Jr., 17, Knoxville, Tennessee; Pier Alexander Shelton, 28, Bremen, Georgia; Lindani Myeni, 29, Honolulu, Hawaii; Innes Lee Jr., 25, Cleveland, Ohio; Roderick Inge, 29, Tuscaloosa, Alabama; Larry Jenkins, 52, Winter Haven, Florida; Ryan Oneal Williams, 31, Fort Worth, Texas; Doward Syleen Baker, 39, Dothan, Alabama; Ma'Khia Bryant, 16, Columbus, Ohio; Andrew Brown, 42, Elizabeth City, North Carolina; Tory Casey, 41, Rosenberg, Texas; Michael Lee McClure, 26, Billings, Montana; Marvin Veiga, 32, Nashville, Tennessee; Hanad Abdiaziz, 25, Kansas City, Missouri; Terrance Maurice Parker, 36, Washington, DC; Eric Derrell Smith, 30, Biloxi, Mississippi; La'Mello Parker, 1, Biloxi, Mississippi; Latoya Denis James, 37, Woodbine, Georgia; Ashton Pinke, 27, Mesquite, Texas; Adonis Traughber, 54, Clarksville, Texas; Kalon Horton, 29, Lancaster, Texas; Lance Lowe, 30, Stockton, California; Monolito Ford, 48, Indianapolis, Indiana; Timothy Fleming, 49, Baltimore, Maryland; Denzell Nathan Clarke, 28, Waldorf, Maryland; Tyrone Penny, 21, Decatur, Georgia; Gary Moncrief, 32, Montgomery, Alabama; Darion M. Lafayette, 24, Champaign, Illinois; Patrick Watkins, 31, Pittsburg, California; Kortnee Lashon Warren, 23, Albany, Georgia; Zaekwon Malik Gullatte-Graves, 25, Houston, Texas; Juan Joseph Daniele Castellano, 38, Athens, Georgia; Darren Dejuan Chandler, 34, Lenexa, Kansas; Shannon Wright, 29, Denver, Colorado; Antonio Christopher Jones, 26, Houston, Texas; Demetrius Stanley, 31, San Jose, California; Bilal Winston Shabazz, 29, Yucca Valley, California; William Brookins Sr., 39, Phoenix, Arizona; Winston Smith, 32, Minneapolis, Minnesota; Andrew Homen, 34, Braintree, Massachusetts; Timothy Flowers, 29, Rochester, New York; Michael Lee Ross Jr., 32, Forest Hill, Texas; Terrell Gas, 36, College Park, Georgia; Josiah L. Byard, 21, Willcox, Arizona; Rezek Yaqub Yahya, 39, Salt Lake City, Utah; Solomon Jamison, 28, Jackson, Mississippi; Jermaine Sonnier, 19, Houston, Texas; Ansy Dolce, 29, Holly Springs, Georgia; Carlos Jackson, 43, Lithia Springs, Georgia; Briana Sykes, 19, Flint, Michigan; Jeff Melvin, 20, Salem, Alabama; De'Shon Hill, 39, Luray, Virginia; Earl Fitzgerald Hunter, 40, Greenville, South Carolina; Fred Holder, 28, Norwalk, California; Albert Wayne Finnie Jr., 22, College Station, Texas; Tristan Trevino, 24, Corpus Christi, Texas; Jerome Barber, 59, Azusa, California; Joseph Lee Humbles, 29, Atlanta, Georgia; Shannon Earl Smith, 45, Spartanburg, South Carolina; John Reuben Turbe, 30, Tampa, Florida; Gulia Dale III, 61, Newton, New Jersey; Klevontaye White, 34, Chicago, Illinois; Justin Powell, 32, Baltimore, Maryland; Marquez Floyd, 31, Albuquerque, New Mexico; Ryan LeRoux,

21, Gaithersburg, Maryland; Maurice Sentel Mincey, 36, Savannah, Georgia; Quentin Bogard, 36, Canton, Mississippi; Leslie Stephen Scarlett, 35, Tucson, Arizona; Irvin Peterson, 35, Houston, Texas; Gabriel "Sam" Parker, 38, Atlanta, Georgia; Losardo Lucas, 55, Calumet City, Illinois; Alexis C. Wilson, 19, Dolton, Illinois; Antonio King, 22, Nashville, Tennessee; Dashawn "Big Top" Batiste, 22, Lafayette, Louisiana; Marcus Martin, 40, Baltimore, Maryland; Christopher Robinson, 48, Seguin, Texas; Antonio Jackson, 27, Memphis, Tennessee; Broderick Shelton, 42, Milwaukee, Wisconsin; Terrence Bey, 29, Philadelphia, Pennsylvania; Devonte Dawayne Brown, 28, Marietta, Georgia; James Matalice Smith, 41, Somerville, Texas; Tyran Lamb, 31, Milwaukee, Wisconsin; Tory Brown, 22, College Park, Georgia; Robert Anderson, 38, Crescent City, California; Antwan Gilmore, 27, Washington, DC; Fanta Bility, 8, Sharon Hill, Pennsylvania; Christopher Corey Moore, 41, Greensboro, North Carolina; Johnny Lee Perry II, 31, Missoula, Montana; Paris Wilder, 38, West Melbourne, Florida; James Williams, 33, Indianapolis, Indiana; Cedric Baxter, 60, Buena Park, California; Frederick Thomas, 41, Miamisburg, Ohio; Josue Arias, 32, Clearwater, Florida; Leden Boykins, 12, Douglasville, Georgia; Cedric Williams, 29, Oxon Hill, Maryland; Desmond Lewis, 30, Shreveport, Louisiana; Tristan Vereen, 33, Longs, South Carolina; Robert Parks, 39, Smyrna, Georgia; Joshua Cooper, 31, Brooklyn, New York; Dishawn Sanders, Jackson, Mississippi; Adrian Cameron, 47, Nashville, Tennessee; Unsfored Lewis Thurmond, 27, Smyrna, Georgia; Turell Brown, 28, Chicago, Illinois; Deon Ledet, 30, Houston, Texas; Desmond Damond Louis, 20, Lake Charles, Louisiana; Keith Cole, 50, Senatobia, Mississippi; Gloria Marie Strong, 27, Allen, Texas; Kyle Anthony Veyon, 26, Columbus, Ohio; Darrion Taylor, 26, Tucson, Arizona; Demetrius Roberts, 21, Las Vegas, Nevada; Corey Daniel Wellman, 40, Nashville, Tennessee; Simran Gordon, 24, Rochester, New York; Ramone Javaris Dwight, 29, Hagan, Georgia; Derrick Clinton, 27, Indian Land, South Carolina; Michael Carothers, 17, Austin, Texas; Jovan Lewis Singleton, 36, Woodlawn, Maryland; Jermaine Harris, 32, Tarboro, North Carolina; Allan Lorenzo Robb, 33, West Palm Beach, Florida; Deandre Johnson, 30, Washington, DC; Johnny McGee, 36, Houma, Louisiana; Name withheld by police, 30, Columbia, Missouri; Steven Thomas, 36, Las Vegas, Nevada; Jabari Farafiai Asante-Chioke, 52, Metairie, Louisiana; Anthony Harden, 30, Fall River, Massachusetts; Lionel Womack, 35, Kansas City, Kansas; Edward Allen Gatling, 38, Lithonia, Georgia, and Anei Joker, 20, Taylorsville, Utah (Rahman, 2021).

So while the promise of opportunities for Black men in America is on the rise, the startling reality is that Black males are in a crisis for their very survival. As of March 3, 2022, Black people are still killed at higher rates than other groups (Bunn, 2022). In addition to being more likely to be murdered by the police, Black males are more likely to be under surveillance by police than any other group (Balcko, 2020), more likely to be arrested than any other group (Health, 2014), once convicted of a crime more likely to have a harsher and longer sentence for the same offense than any other group (Palazzolo, 2013), and more likely to be expelled and suspended from school than any other group (Superintendent's Educational Opportunity Advisory Council, 2013; Zill & Wilcox, 2019). With regard to employment, the only time a Black male has the same chance of getting a job as a White male is if he has a master's degree and the White male has no degree (Blesser, 2014; Johnson, 2019). If a Black male is hired, he typically earns a lower wage than White males in the same position. In the rare instances where the media and supporters of civil rights collaborate to protest police brutality against Black males such as with the Black Lives Matter campaign, opponents often assert that these protests negatively impact police officers (Blinder, 2015). What are the circumstances behind these facts? And what prompted America to simultaneously extol Black males and exile them at the same time? This book attempts to answer some of these questions and start conversations that lead to solutions. We begin with one of the most influential concerns that affect Black males: social factors related to education outcomes. But first, a brief exercise to help ground the reader with reflective mindful questions.

BEGINNING REFLECTION

Mindful Teaching Practices for Black Male Achievement was created to help you have better relationships with Black male students. Please find a quiet place where you are comfortable as well as relaxed and free to write your answers to each of these questions for at least twenty minutes without concern for grammar or punctuation. If you need more room, just find a piece of paper and continue!

Write about yourself, that is, are you a teacher, a principal, a superintendent, a parent, a community member, a policymaker? Other?

What matters most in your life (family, friendships, career, etc.)?

What is your role (an educator, a healer, an advisor, a mentor, a sister, a friend of a Black male, or other)?

What is one thing you would like Black male students to know about you?

What would you like to know about Black males?

We'll come back to these questions later.

Chapter 1

Social Factors that Influence Educational Outcomes

 Before the Civil War, there wasn't a free school in the state, but under the Reconstruction government, we built them in every county. . . . We paid to have every child, Negro and White schooled equally

—George Washington Albright (1937)

DWENNIMMEN, HUMILITY, AND STRENGTH

Vignette

My Name Is Theodore

My name is important because had my name been Tyrone, Jamal, or Winston, my life outcomes may have been a little bit different. Because my first name is Theodore, no one knows what my race is on job applications, and no one knows what my race is on my college application or when I applied to graduate school. I was able to pay for college by working in restaurants. There is typically not a lot of Black males who work in front of the house in restaurants, so when people look at my resume . . . when they see my name is Theodore, it doesn't necessarily occur to them that I'm Black. I've gone to restaurant interviews where I've walked in, and when they saw me, they said, "You are Theodore?" They looked down at my resume, and then looked back up at me and said, "Well . . . okay," and proceed with the interview. So what I'm talking about is perception. When review committees looked at my PhD program application or when I looked for a job after I graduated with my doctorate, "Theodore" sounds like someone who'd be a professor. In other words,

I'm saying that perception is everything, and because the name "Theodore" isn't perceived as someone who is Black, my life has been a lot easier for me than others who had non-White ethnic-sounding names.

Educators and policymakers have continually looked for ways to improve educational outcomes for Black male students. We begin with an obvious issue: social factors that impact schooling. A guiding question for this first chapter is: *What are the ways that gender, culture, and race impact learning?*

MALE LEARNING STYLES

Regarding male and female learning styles, there are two main streams of thought: biological and cultural (Ransaw, 2013). The biological stream supports the belief that the brains of males and females are just wired differently (Pescale & Primavera, 2019). For boys, in general, their cerebral cortex is dedicated to spatial awareness. Boys also have less oxytocin and serotonin in their brain than girls, the hormones that help bring on a sense of calm (Zamosky, 2011). However, boys do have higher levels of testosterone and dopamine in their blood, which is known to increase impulse behavior and physical activity (Laube, Lorenz, & van den Bos, 2020). The second school of thought regarding males and females is that learning is influenced by cultural factors. Put simply, some believe that boys are socialized into gender roles that are more physical than intellectual (Ransaw & Green, 2016). These messages, which focus on being tough, independent, and self-resilient, make it difficult for boys to ask for help. Some researchers call this cultural conditioning the "boy code" (Cleveland, 2011). The boy code is both the formal and informal messages that males receive regarding acceptable male behavior in society (Pollack, 1998). Some believe that being male is a practice that is recreated under constantly changing social conditions (Wedgwood, 2009) and is not a fixed biological behavior (Ransaw, 2013). Schools are environments that often sustain social and cultural masculine behavior in the classroom.

THE PRAXIS OF COOL IN THE CLASSROOM

A combination of attributes related to self-resolve and resistance to oppression that Blacks have shown in their personal and collective existence "coolness" stems from a powerful influence known as *ashe* (De La Casa, 1994; Bascom, 1969). *Ashe* (pronounced ash-heh) is a Yoruba term from West Africa that is related to character. Someone who has *ashe* has the power to make things happen despite the odds. In other words, *ashe* can be a source of inner strength, a nonviolent, confident cool form of resistance against oppression (De La Casa, 1994).

Black boys construct their Black masculinity based on what they expect from themselves to survive physically and emotionally (hooks, 2004; Franklin, 1985). This definition of Black masculinity is often called *cool pose* (Majors & Billson, 1992) and can result in a withdrawal from study and immersion into sports. This balancing act between being social and being scholarly is an attempt to find a "middle way" between schoolwork and "cool work" in order to be socially accepted (Frosh, Phoenix, & Pattman, 2002, p. 205). To avoid being perceived as uncool, many boys who are successful in school sometimes try to make it look effortless (Jackson & Dempster, 2009). In fact, some boys hide their books in their lunch bags or pretend not to study at all to fit in.

So in essence, the effortless demonstration of masculinity also known as being cool can be viewed as a cultural archetype (Jung, 1966), significantly intersecting class with race, sexuality, gender, and nationality (Connell, 2000), and related to ideology and interpersonal relationships in adolescent ethnic identity (Wilson et al., 2010; Steinberg, 1993). Cool is the performance of masculinity based on looking relaxed and effortless. A relatable and approachable teacher who helps Black males balance their academic capital and social capital can use this *cool factor* to build bridges to improve educational outcomes (Ransaw, 2013).

PERCEPTIONS

Black males are typically thought of as aggressive, violent, and not well behaved. The negative images of Black males are so embedded and pervasive in our culture that they are also perceived as unemployed, uneducated, and uneducable (Ransaw, 2014). Unfavorable perceptions of Black males are so persistent that the way they walk, talk, and even their names can be barriers to them in school (Ransaw, 2013). Even the walk or stroll—the tendency of African American males to swagger—has forced teachers to consider Black boys more likely to attain lower academic achievement, to need special educational attention, and to act aggressively (Neal et al., 2003). These negative perceptions, which often lead to suspensions and expulsions of Black males, start as early as the second week in preschool (CBS News, 2014). Common solutions that are known to improve Black male achievement and counter negative perceptions are rite of passage initiatives and mentorship programs (Ransaw, 2013).

RITES OF PASSAGE AND MENTORING

In most African tribes, mentoring starts after a rite of passage. In rites of passage, the focus is on *separation*, where plebs (initiates) are set apart from the ordinary. These beginners engage in rites of separation or *acts of transition*, also called "*marge* or limen," which incorporate the threshold or simultaneously occupied spaces between past, present, and future. Young men-to-be also engage in rites of initiation—*aggregation*—in which youths are reintroduced to society as full members (van Gennep, 1960). This ritual is similar to "passing the line" rituals when initiates become full members of a fraternity. A precursor to Greek fraternities, African shield groups are divisions of men within a tribe composed of elder warriors (senior advisors) who mentor the new incoming warriors (mentees) after they have finished their rites of passage. One of the most famous African tribes that utilizes shield groups is the Zulu people.

During the 1960s in the New York borough of the Bronx, a young Black boy named Lance Taylor entered an essay contest and won a trip to Africa as his prize. While in Africa, Lance met a Zulu tribal leader who inspired him to unite with other Black males in New York for political and economic power. Lance soon after changed his name to Afrika Bambaataa Asim, a derivative of the Zulu Chief Bambaataa who led an armed rebellion in South Africa. Bambaataa did indeed network with other Black males in the Bronx. Together, Bambaataa (Bam); Joseph Saddler, known as Grandmaster Flash (Flash); and Clive Campbell, DJ Kool Hercules (Herc), are known as the founding fathers of hip-hop, a cultural movement that spread from New York across the world (George, 2014). Bam, Flash, and Herc can be thought of as tribal leaders who inspired an entire generation to create a fresh culture that became a unifying voice to teach others using a structured culture that spoke and expressed itself through social learning.

HIP-HOP

Hip-hop is a form of popular music that originated among inner-city African American youth in the 1980s, drawing on Jamaican rhythms, funk, street sounds, and fragments of melody and rhythm borrowed from previously recorded sources. Hip-hop can be effectively divided and analyzed into four distinct "families" or genres: graffiti, b-boying, D-jaying, and rap. In an article by Bonz Malone for *Source Magazine*, hip-hop originator and innovator Richie Colon, better known as Crazy Legs, describes the four elements or "children" of hip-hop: "Graffiti is the Black Sheep. B-boying is the bastard child of hip-hop. D-Jaying is the loyal child who always does what he is told. Rap is the spoiled brat who is actually the youngest of the four" (Malone, 2003, p. 132). Hip-hop has become a means of communication, self-expression, and identity for many youths in America. The genre of hip-hop has also been a means of financial success for many entrepreneurs as well as a source of exploitation by the media and corporations by simultaneously promoting both positive and negative images of Black males (Ransaw, 2013). Rapper Chuck D of the hip-hop group Public Enemy said that rap was Black America's *CNN* because it educates and communicates the way Blacks think and feel (Eichler, 2010). Educators often find success when they let Black students express themselves through hip-hop in their lessons and assignments.

The impact of hip-hop on Black culture and Black education cannot be overstated as Blacks have worked to educate each other while American schooling has failed and continues to fail Blacks in America. America at one time made it illegal to teach Blacks how to read and jailed or administered corporal punishment to Whites who taught them (North Carolina General Assembly, 1830). In short, Blacks in America had to learn to teach themselves. Black social learning is not just restricted to music genres but also includes formal learning at HBCUs.

BLACK COLLEGES

An HBCU is defined as any "Historically Black College or University that was established prior to 1964, whose principal mission was, and is, the education of Black Americans" (US Department of Education, 2009, p. 1). HBCUs were important then because, before 1865, there was a prohibition against educating Blacks. However, by the 1950s HBCUs had become the overwhelming provider of education for Black lawyers, Black doctors, Black teachers, and other types of Black community leaders (Roebuck & Murty 1993). Lerone Bennett Jr. in Thomas and Green's (2001) introduction said, "If Historically Black Colleges and Universities did not exist in their present form, it would be necessary for the supporters of Black educational excellence to re-invent them" (p. 245).

As of 2020, HBCUs are the higher institutions that have the greatest success preparing Blacks for careers in science and awarded 13 percent of bachelor's degrees and 6 percent of master's degrees in 2018 (Wildener, 2020; National Center for Education Statistics, 2020). According to a 2015 report, Black HBCU graduates are more likely to be thriving in financial, purpose, and well-being than Black graduates from other institutions (Finley, 2015). Also of note, Zethena Prince and Trice Edney (2015) report that Black HBCU graduates feel better supported and more prepared for life after college than Black students who did not attend an HBCU.

Although HBCUs only make up around 3 percent of US colleges and universities, they graduate nearly 20 percent of all American college graduates (Borrelli, 2021). Additionally, HBCUs accept students who have lower test scores as well as students who are more likely to come from poor homes (Elfman, 2019). Because HBCUs provide more opportunities for Black male students to interact with Black faculty, they have higher graduation rates for Black men (Gates, 2019). The takeaway here is that Black males thrive when they are given both academic and social support that includes having a close relationship with faculty and teachers.

This chapter provided a concise overview of social factors that influence educational outcomes. We began with this topic because all too often well-meaning and curious Black males suffer indignities in the classroom through no fault of their own. However, the intent is not to imply that social factors alone are the cause of poor educational outcomes for Black males in American schools. There are other issues such as zero-tolerance policies that negatively affect Black male educational outcomes. Chapter 2 provides additional insights into other concerns that move beyond zero-tolerance policies such as the school-to-prison pipeline and the prison industrial complex.

CHAPTER 1 REFLECTION

Social Factors that Influence Educational Outcomes

Guiding Question: *What are the ways that gender, culture, and race affect learning?*

In a relaxed and comfortable place, free write your answers to each of the questions for at least five minutes without concern for grammar or punctuation. If you need more room, just find another piece of paper and continue!

Reflections

Have you ever had a Black male student with whom you wish you had a better connection?

How does the fact that you didn't make the connection you wanted to make you feel?

What do you think is the nature of the disconnection?

Did any of the topics in this chapter highlighted on race, culture, or gender play a role in the disconnect?

Is there any way to make connections based on the information you've learned in the chapter or in other ways you haven't thought of yet?

What are your most important takeaways from this chapter?

Prolepsis

Imagine that you are at least five years in the future. The Black male student in the previous example is giving the class graduation speech and has recommended that you introduce him. As you step out to walk onto the podium, you think about the day you met him and where he is today. Your heart is warmed because you played a role in his success. How did the two of you get to this moment? And what was your plan to make it happen?

Chapter 2

Social and Institutional Policies that Affect Educational Outcomes

 The thought of the inferiority of the Negro is drilled into him in almost every class he enters and in almost every book he studies.

—Carter G. Woodson (1933/1990)

EPA, LAW, AND JUSTICE COMPLEXITIES OF LIFE

Vignette

Accidental Outcomes

I was never particularly a good student in school. I used to get into trouble for fooling around or talking too much, especially during reading. I would always read my assignments. But then I would bug the students around me when I was bored. My reading teacher, Mr. Thompson, would say, "Hey, stop fooling around and get back to work—finish your reading assignment!" I would say, "I did finish reading." And he would say, "Then read it again!" I would read it again. But on the next day, we would repeat the same thing. One day, I thought I was outsmarting Mr. Thompson when I told him that I had read my reading assignment twice. But my strategy didn't work. Soon I was reading my assignments three times a day. That was until Mr. Thompson called me to his desk one day and asked me if I wanted to go to the reading van. The reading van was a special bus project funded by the city to increase literacy. The reading van came by our school twice a week on Tuesdays and Thursdays. I said "yes" to the reading van because it meant that I would get out of class for a couple of hours. The following week, the reading van came by, and the teacher in charge gave me a reading test. Afterward, he looked at me and said, "You don't have any problems with reading!" I responded, "I never said that I had problems with reading. Does that mean I have to go back to class now?" He said, "No." He gave me a book to read for the rest of the hour. On his next visit, he started giving me college prep material. It turned out that, when I was in junior high school, I had a college reading level and college reading comprehension level. The reading van teacher also visited high schools when he wasn't at my school and just let me use the resources he already had around. If it weren't for me being sent to the reading van because I was a troublemaker, I would never have known that I was smart, and I would never have had a chance to take college prep classes in junior high school. A good teacher can make a difference.

Now that you have a better understanding of the social issues that are related to educational outcomes, we will take a closer look at the way society creates policies that affect educational outcomes and the reasons behind them. The guiding questions for this chapter are: *"Is the American education system operating the way it was intended to?"* and *"Why, or why not? Do you think so?"*

OBSTACLES AND OPPORTUNITY

America has a history of placing policy barriers to quality education for African Americans, and it began with the institution of slavery. Blacks did not participate in integrated schools until the 1954 *Brown v. Board of Education of Topeka* US Supreme Court decision to desegregate schools. This overruled the *Plessy v. Ferguson* 1896 decision to allow the so-called separate but equal schooling between Blacks and Whites (Lawnix, 2014). Not only were there separate schools for Blacks at one time in the United States, but it was also considered constitutional to have separate bathrooms, separate water fountains, and separate transportation. Popularly known as Jim Crow Laws, segregation resulted in the practice of unequal education for Blacks in the United States. These disparities continued into other areas of Black/White social relations until *Brown v. Board of Education*. However, that ruling resulted in many parts of the country resisting integration, eliminating funding for schools in Black neighborhoods, and leaving many Black students without a source of education (Smith, 1965). This resulted in the 1955 *Brown v. Board of Education II* that mandated desegregation be implemented with all deliberate speed. Garry Orfield's (1999) research asserts that, despite this ruling, the case was reopened again in the 1978 *Brown v. Board of Education III* to prevent White parents from sending their children to predominantly White and/

or private schools (Orfield & Yun, 1999). In other words, many White parents did not want their children to go to the same schools as Black children.

RESISTANCE AND RESILIENCE TO
EDUCATE BLACK MALES

There is a long history of denying education to Blacks in the United States. For example, in 1827, Frederick Douglass heard his owner scold his wife and reprimand her for teaching him how to read the Bible. As Douglass (1852/2006) recounts in his *What, to the Slave, Is the Fourth of July?*, "If you teach that n***** how to read, there would be no keeping him," and he would "become unmanageable, and of no value to his master" (p. 33). While the incident of 1827 involved just a verbal punishment, by 1831, a bill was passed preventing slaves from learning how to read and write and was later enforced by imprisonment. Among the individuals punished for this "offense," Prudence Crandall was placed in jail for educating Blacks in 1834, and Mrs. Margaret Douglass of Norfolk, Virginia, was placed in prison for teaching Blacks how to read in 1853 (North Carolina Digital History, 2010). Today, schools are open to Black children. But being open to Black students attending a school is not the same thing as creating policies to keep them in school. Far too many Black children, especially Black male students, are kicked out and pushed out of school based on zero-tolerance policies.

ZERO-TOLERANCE POLICIES

In 1982, Nancy Reagan responded to a question of what to do when someone offers you drugs by saying, "Just say no." This phrase became a campaign slogan for the war on drugs because of its zero-tolerance perspective on drug use and then later guns. Zero-tolerance policies are predetermined consequences regardless of the severity of the infraction including everything from minor infractions to major offences (Wald & Losen, 2003). Zero-tolerance policies gained favor because they gave the appearance that schools were tough on crime. However, zero-tolerance policies became subjective rules to police students and had detrimental effects on all students, but especially harmed Black students. For instance, one student was kicked out of school for chewing his Pop-Tart into the shape of a gun (Burris, 2013). And as you can imagine, zero-tolerance policies were extended to include drugs. An eighth grader was arrested for taking Tylenol for a headache, thereby breaking the school's no drug policy (ACLU, 2001).

SCHOOL-TO-PRISON PIPELINE

Aggressive enforcement policies like zero tolerance led to increased suspensions and expulsions that often lead to incarceration, hence the term "school-to-prison pipeline." Once a student has a juvenile suspension record, his likelihood of graduating on time decreases while the circumstances that lead to prison incarceration increase (Rampey et al., 2016).

Not only are students marked as potential troublemakers after a suspension or expulsion, but it was not uncommon for students to be targeted and placed on high surveillance by both truant officers and school-assigned police officers (American Civil Liberties Union, 2017). In Las Vegas, Nevada, after suffering heavy surveillance, Black males are disproportionately placed on gang lists, making it difficult for them to get jobs after turning eighteen (Lombardo, 2015). In fact, students placed on gang lists must petition to be taken off such a list. Overall, the zero-tolerance policies had an unfavorable impact on students of color through no fault of their own other than their skin color.

"Data have consistently shown that the over-representation of students of color in school discipline rates is not due to higher rates of misbehavior by these students, but instead is driven by structural and systemic factors" (US Commission on Civil Rights, 2019, p. 4). The more classes students miss because of detentions, suspensions, and expulsions, the fewer opportunities they have to learn.

JUVENILE INCARCERATION

Juvenile incarceration decreases the probability of high-school graduation. For example, junior high-school dropouts are 3.5 times more likely to be arrested than high-school dropouts, and 63 percent more likely to be incarcerated than peers with four-year degrees (Literacy, Mid-South, 2016). Concerning Black youth specifically, out of 100,000 incarcerated youth, Black youth incarceration was 433 compared to just 86 for White youth (Equal Justice Initiative, 2017). In 2017, Black boys were placed in the juvenile justice system at a rate of 43 percent, while Black children only make up 14 percent of all Americans under the age of eighteen (Serrano, 2018). It is important to note that if a student is not reading proficiently in fourth grade, they have a 70 percent chance of not catching up and falling behind (Rampey et al., 2016). Regarding mathematics, not taking the right math classes in the right sequence is a leading cause of achievement gaps (Schmidt, 2015; US Department of Education, 2018). Opportunities to learn are diminished the more classes a student misses.

These dire circumstances are combined to make some schools an environment where students feel that there is little hope and then drop out because of a lack of opportunity for a quality education that could improve their lives. The importance of understanding how the link between exclusionary schooling, inequitable housing, poor health, and incarceration are linked to everyday life for minority communities cannot be overstated.

PRISON INDUSTRIAL COMPLEX

The prison industrial complex describes "the overlapping interests of government and industry that use surveillance, policing, and imprisonment as solutions to economic, social and political problems" (Critical Resistance, 2015). Here in the United States, we are imprisoning more people than ever before. In fact, the United States incarcerates more people than any other country in the world (Lee, 2015). What is more alarming is that, in 2019, African Americans were incarcerated at a higher rate than any other ethnic group in the country (Statista, 2021). In 2019, African Americans were incarcerated at a rate of 600 incarcerations per 100,000 people, American Indian/Alaskan Native 420 per 100,000 people, Whites 184 per 100,000 people, and Asians 25 per 100,000 people (Statista, 2021).

The incarceration of people in the United States has a long historical tradition. Acts of labor exploitation of people who were incarcerated, under indentured servitude, or enslaved were prevalent almost from the very beginning of American history.

According to Bauer (2020), in the 1700s, British convicts were sold to America as laborers. By the mid-1800s Louisiana privatized its state penitentiaries and put inmates to work in factories, and children born to Blacks who were in the penitentiary serving life sentences became state property. When slavery and indentured servitude were abolished in 1865 by the Thirteenth Amendment, free labor was legally allowed through prison labor. In it, the Thirteenth Amendment stated: "Neither slavery nor involuntary servitude, except as a punishment for crime whereof the party shall have been duly convicted, shall exist within the United States, or any place subject to their jurisdiction" (US Const., amend. XIII).

Former slave owners were able to make false claims of criminal activity of formerly enslaved Blacks and conscript them to slave labor on prison chain gangs. In fact, a large part of the land that former slave owners held in Alabama, Arkansas, Mississippi, Tennessee, Texas, and Louisiana was sold and used to build prisons. Described by Van Jones as "slave ships on dry land" (V. Jones, 2007; Reiland, 2009), this is the land to which enslaved people came to America on ships as captives and on which they were forced to plant, pick, and harvest crops. This same land has become the land on which crops are planted, picked, and harvested by enslaved prison inmates who are now incarcerated captives.

Then as now, prisons do not have to pay inmates a proper salary. This makes workers who are incarcerated particularly desirable to exploit. For example, in one Texas prison, prisoners manufacture the razor wire on the fences surrounding the prison; they also manufacture the janitorial supplies; grow the cotton and weave it into the fabrics used for prison uniforms, towels, and blankets; and even manufacture the toothpaste they use. Put simply, prison labor is cheap, affordable, and therefore easy to profit from. Companies that utilize prison labor include Whole Foods, McDonald's, Starbucks, Verizon, AT&T, Fidelity Investments, and American Airlines (Gutierrez, 2020). As long as Black boys are pushed out of school, making it easier for them to become incarcerated in juvenile detention, thereby making it more likely that they become incarcerated Black male adults who provide affordable labor, some members of society will always be tempted to utilize zero-tolerance policies.

This chapter provided an overview of social factors that influence educational outcomes. We began with this topic because all too often well-meaning, bright, and curious Black males suffer indignities in the classroom through no fault of their own. However, the intent of this chapter is not to imply that social factors alone are the cause of poor educational outcomes for Black males. There are other issues such as zero-tolerance policies that negatively affect Black males. Chapter 3 provides additional insights into other schools of concerns that move beyond zero-tolerance policies, the school-to-prison pipeline, and the prison industrial complex by highlighting the impacts negative perceptions and negative thinking have on Black male students' educational outcomes.

CHAPTER 2 REFLECTIONS

Social and Institutional Policies that Affect Educational Outcomes

Guiding Question: *Is the American education system operating the way it was intended to? Why or why not? Do you think so?*

In a relaxed and comfortable place, free write your answers to each of the questions for at least five minutes without concern for grammar or punctuation. If you need more room, just find another piece of paper and continue!

Reflections

Do you think that the American education system is equitable for all students?
How does your answer make you feel?
Do you think the American education system was designed to be equitable?
How does your answer make you feel?
What are your most important takeaways from this chapter?

Prolepsis

Imagine the year is 2041. In 2041, there are no achievement gaps or missed educational opportunities for Black males. What did it take to make schools equitable? What was your plan to make schools equitable? Describe in detail how your plan helped.

Positive and Negative Thinking that Impact Perception and Performance

We must eradicate the slander that says a Black youth with a book is acting white.

—Barack Obama (2004)

ANANSE NTONTAN, WISDOM, CREATIVITY, AND THE COMPLEXITIES OF LIFE

Vignette

Perfect Score

When I was the director of a mentorship program for an at-risk elementary school, a student was recommended to the mentorship program because he was frequently absent. He never came to school on Mondays or Tuesdays and was always in trouble for low attendance. We let the mentees pick out whatever book they wanted to read. He picked out a book that was way above his grade level. It was about Black inventors. I thought to myself, "If he's interested in reading it, what could be the harm?" At the end of the year, he had to take his grade-level assessments as all students do. On his reading exam, he got a perfect score. His teachers and school board members didn't believe it. They made the principal administer the test a second time, and again, he got another perfect score. So not only did he make community members angry because he was getting good grades while having low attendance, now he's on record for getting a perfect reading score twice. At risk does not mean count students out.

So far in this book, we have looked at social factors that influence educational outcomes. This chapter will look at an additional factor that impacts the lives of Black males: a positive mind-set. Thinking positively is an asset for all of us. A guiding question for this chapter is: *What would the Black males that you know achieve if they thought they could do anything?*

It may be possible that psychology researchers are not racist, report the facts as they determine them, and may not have any ill intent at all. However, it is worth noting that human psychology and behavioral science journals typically include research participants from Western, educated, industrialized, rich, and Democratic societies (WEIRD) (Henrich, Heine, & Norenzayan, 2010). The fact that psychology research is based on population samples that are not representative of the ethnicity, education level, occupation, income level, and political affiliation of people who do not represent the majority of the world's population means that psychological and behavioral interpretations are being made without all of the facts. Numerous aspects of what it means to be human—visual perception, sense of fairness, attitude toward cooperation, spatial reasoning, categorization, inferential induction, moral reasoning, reasoning styles, self-concept, and motivations—vary by population (Henrich, Heine, & Norenzayan, 2010). Consequently, there are fundamental biases and misconceptions about race and human behavior.

However, the problem of the lack of racial inclusion in psychology research does not just end with participant bias. According to Roberts, Bareket-Shavit, Dollins, Goldie, and Mortenson (2020), 83 percent of the editors in chief of the top two journals of cognitive psychology were White, and only 5 percent were people of color. Additionally, between the 1970s and the 2010s, fewer than 0.01 percent of cognitive psychology journals looked at race, and only 8 percent of development psychology journals and 8 percent of special psychology journals focused on race. Additionally, White editors publish fewer articles about people of color than editors of color at a ratio of 4 percent to 11 percent, respectively. Even more surprisingly, 87 percent of academic publications in their study were edited by White editors (Roberts et al., 2020). To summarize, people of color are not represented by the researchers, participants, and editors of psychology journals. Consequently, Black male students are perceived through the lens of non-Black standards.

Historically, psychologists in the United States have been biased toward Blacks. For example, it was once thought that Blacks enjoyed being slaves.

For those who criticized slavery because of its harmful effect on the Negro, Cartwright had a ready answer. The Negro, he said, found positive pleasure in laboring in the hot sun. Furthermore, there was no danger of overworking him; for unlike the white man who like a "full-blooded horse" could be worked to death—the Negro, "like the mule," could not be overworked. "The white men of America," Cartwright said, had "performed many prodigies," but they had "never yet been able to make a negro overwork himself." (Cartwright, 1858, p. 222)

It was also once thought that Blacks enjoyed being enslaved so much that if they did run away, they must have had a mental disease called drapetomania. Today, conversations about race are so connected to racism, prejudice, and bias that it is difficult and painful for many Whites to even talk about it, much less discuss it.

Sociology professor Ron Eyerman (2001) calls the syndrome where a collective has been subject to an unbearable event or experience that undermines their sense of group identity, values, meaning, purpose, or cultural worldviews "cultural trauma." Cultural trauma is used frequently in conversations when scholars talk about Indigenous populations and members of the Diaspora (peoples of African descent who were enslaved in the New World). Subsequently, the residual cultural trauma experienced during and after the Diaspora can cause posttraumatic slave syndrome (PTSS) (DeGruy, 2005).

POSTTRAUMATIC SLAVE SYNDROME

Assistant professor and sociologist Joy DeGruy (2005) is most known for her work on PTSS, a theory that describes slavery's multigenerational effect on African Americans. DeGruy asserts that PTSS causes those affected to have feelings of a foreshortened future, an exaggerated startle response, and an increase of hypervigilance in threatening situations. PTSS is also responsible for feelings of hopelessness and depression. It may also be wise to keep in mind the fact that there was no psychotherapy during slavery, either from the treatment of being enslaved or the sale and/or displacement of children. PTSS differs from PTSD in that PTSS conceptualizes the neurochemical reactions to stress as something that continues for generations. Freud (1939) described intergenerational trauma as phylogenetic inheritance, "the mental residue . . ., with each new generation, needs only to be awakened, not reacquired."

Anti-Black Racism

Anti-Blackness, also known as anti-Black racism, is characterized as both physical hostility and formal (policy) and informal (mistreatment toward Blacks considered normalthat is, Jim Crow Laws) discrimination including in housing, education, health care, policy, as well as characterizing experiences of violence and harassment (United Nations, 2013). A concrete definition of anti-Blackness was necessary so that the numerous negative actions toward Blacks could be addressed by the United Nations to identify the issues impacting people of African descent and to help find solutions.

Afrophobia

Another racial phenomenon that targets people with Black skin is Afrophobia. While anti-Blackness is racism directed toward anyone of African descent, Afrophobia is rooted in the thinking of Africans as unworthy to be called human because they represent an unvalued country. At first glance, anti-Blackness and Afrophobia seem to be the same. A closer look reveals the extent of the complexity of racism directed toward Black people and Black people who live in Africa.

> Whereby anti-blackness is fixated and rooted more deeply in historical power dynamics and the perpetual White subjugation over Black bodies, Afrophobia permeates a deeper level and merges this historical positioning of the Black other as subordinate with more continent specific realities, such as backwardness, poverty, and disease. (Ntinu, 2019, p. 14)

Ntinu's (2019) definition of Afrophobia highlights the intersectionality of being a member of the Black race and separated Black ethnic identity from Black/African geographic location. While anti-Blackness is typically envisioned as systematic discrimination based on housing, economics, health care, and education directed toward *African* Americans, Afrophobia is specifically framed toward the oppression of native *Black* Africans based on the ideology that Africa is backward, illiterate, and poverty ridden (Ntinu, 2019). Afrophobia can be viewed as a form of anti-Blackness of people from colonized Africans, including natives. Afrophobia gives discursive and intellectual space for discussion of Black racism and discrimination based on the particularities specific to the places they live.

Asset Thinking

Afrocentricity

Influential African American professor and philosopher Molefi Kete Asante is most famously known for his creation of the theoretical framework Afrocentricity. Afrocentricity is an African and African American construct that continuously places Black consciousness at the center of its ideology. A trope of both thought and action, Afrocentricity is dedicated to resisting oppression and promoting the idea that African consciousness should be the force behind Black political and social actions (Asante, 2003). One step removed from freedom of education, Afrocentricity is a theory that enables a person to reject European-framed knowledge-based systems in favor of other types of truths. In other words, Africans and African Americans can become sovereign individuals rather than the objects of European education (Asante, 2003). Looking at those of African descent as active participants in history instead of merely as oppressed individuals creates a conversation that is both self-reflective and empowering.

Double Consciousness

It is reasonable to assume that William Edward Burghardt Du Bois (Du Bois, pronounced, Du with u as in Sue; Bois, as oi in voice with the accent is on the second syllable) was highly influenced by Douglass for his articulation of nationalism and race. The idea that Blacks in America are able to look at the American experience with a "divided self," giving them the ability to see the world through multiracial eyes, Du Bois called double consciousness (Du Bois, 1903). This racial intuitiveness enables the oppressed the ability to see society from a unique moral perspective. Double consciousness, an outcome of slavery, empowered those who struggled with the residual impact of being in bondage with a critical perspective of American identity. Du Bois saw that the reflective practice of double consciousness provided a way of looking at the world both in terms of the oppressor and in terms of the oppressed. For Du Bois double consciousness serves as a critical process and awareness of race relations from a moral perspective (Du Bois, 1903). Black French nationals also made connections between race and identity in much the same way as Du Bois.

Négritude

In the 1920s, three Black male students from three different French colonies, Aimé Césaire from Martinique, Léon Gontran Damas from Guiana, and Léopold Sédar Senghor from Senegal, articulated what other Black writers, authors, poets, and scholars conceptualized as Négritude. Négritude is the "affirmation of consciousness of the values of Black or African culture, heritage, and identity" (Bachir, 2018). The Négritude movement used the language of their oppressor, French, to center their Black experience. In fact, French/West Indian psychiatrist and philosopher Frantz Omar Fanon, also known as Ibrahim Frantz Fanon, suggests that language is a form of colonization (Fanon, 1967), so using language as a form of liberation is only fitting. Not surprisingly, Fanon studied under Césaire. Négritude borrows from Du Bois's reflective process of utilizing language and understanding duality to affirm positive Black identity from a Black French perspective (Nielsen,

2013). Practitioners of Négritude also supported Black thought in the form of artistic means such as speech, poetry, and art.

Resiliency

Resilience is "the strengths that people and systems demonstrate that enable them to rise above adversity" (Van Breda, 2001, p. 14). High future expectations are an indicator of resilience.

High Expectations

Dr. Green (2014) asserts that high expectations, the belief that all students can achieve, are a proven tool for successfully teaching African American males. While seemingly obvious, high expectations are important to the development of Black males and subsequent teacher interactions with them because having positive beliefs actually increases productivity (Dweck, 2013). Hattie (2012) asserts that not only does research support the idea that high expectations increase achievement outcomes but also that both high- and lower-performing students appreciate when teachers set equal high expectations for them and their peers. However, according to Milner and Howard (2004), for Black students, high expectations alone are not enough. Having high expectations is more powerful when teachers believe in and identify with their students based on shared common experiences (Milner & Howard, 2004). What researchers are suggesting is that having high expectations opens up both the teachers' and students' mind-sets to be receptive to possibilities. Simply put, positive thinking gets better results.

Positive thinking also increases one's self-esteem, improves self-efficacy, and fosters self-confidence.

Self-Esteem, Self-Efficacy, and Self-Confidence

Identity is composed of at least three components: self-concept, self-esteem, and self-efficacy (Nunez & Loos-Sant'Ana, 2015). Self-concept is a cognitive understanding of habits, experiences, abilities, and feelings including self-reflection and feedback from others. Self-esteem relates to a person's sense of self-worth, and self-efficacy relates to a person's perception of their ability to reach a goal. Additionally, positive self-esteem has also been known to have a direct relationship to self-confidence (Green, 2014).

Deficit Thinking

Deficit thinking is defined as a form of blaming the victim, especially minority students for failures in school. Deficit thinking suggests that poverty, inadequate home life, and poor parenting disrupt learning in the classroom and result in students having limited intelligence, no motivation, and poor social skills (Valencia, 1997; Davis & Museus, 2019). Put simply, deficit thinking centers on school failure as stemming from the minds, bodies, and communities as well as culture of students and pathologies of the language and culture of people who live in poverty (Dudley-Marling, 2015). For some teachers, it is far too easy to fall into the trap of deficit thinking when they do not live in or are not from the communities in which they teach.

At Risk

The National Institute on Education of At-risk Students (1992) defines at-risk students as those students who are vulnerable because of "limited English proficiency, poverty, race, geographic location, or economic disadvantage, who face a greater risk of low educational achievement or reduced academic expectations." This definition has resulted in negative perceptions and low expectations of entire groups of students, typically minority students, and often negatively affects Black male students. An example of nondeficit thinking is describing Black males as students who are the most "at-promise instead of being at-risk" (Haefeli, 2020).

Assumicide

Although originally created by Patty Harty for the investment industry to mean inflated opinion and unreasonable demands, assumicide has been expanded by Bambi Betty for use in the field of education. The most common forms of assumicide are (1) the assumption that the more I talk, the more they will learn; (2) the assumption that surely someone else has already taught this to these kids—it's not my job; (3) the assumption that assigning work is the same as teaching; (4) the assumption that all teachers know how to write effective curriculum; and (5) the assumption that most learning can be assessed through traditional instruments (Betty, 2015).

Microaggression

Microaggressions come in at least three forms: "microassault, microinsult, and microinvalidation" (Sue et al., 2007, p. 271). Racial microaggressions are brief verbal and nonverbal behaviors typically directed toward people of color and often committed without intentional awareness. An example of a racial microaggression is when a teacher mispronounces an ethnic-sounding name and laughs or other students in the class laugh and make fun of how the name sounds. Although it may not have been intentional, laughing at a different-sounding name is an example of an everyday occurrence that has subtle implications. European-sounding names such as Schuyler and

McDuffie are just as difficult to pronounce as Black "ethnic"-sounding names like Tyrone or Lucretia. Making fun of an ethnic-sounding name is increasingly confusing when you realize that Tyrone is both Greek and Irish while Lucretia is a Quaker name with no African origins at all. Understanding the impact of negative perception Black males can experience helps provide a context for the Black male experience and helps amplify the importance of positive thinking when working with Black male students.

An affirming mind-set and positive thinking are both mental states that can positively affect a Black male's outlook on life. Thinking positively also improves a Black male's health. Sadly, not all Black males are invulnerable to mental health issues. Chapter 4 explores a sensitive issue related to Black male health that is not discussed often enough: Black male depression.

CHAPTER 3 REFLECTION

Positive and Negative Thinking that Impacts Perception and Performance Reflections

Guiding Question: *What would the Black males that you know achieve if they thought they could do anything?*

In a relaxed and comfortable place, free write your answers to each of the questions for at least five minutes without concern for grammar or punctuation. If you need more room, just find another piece of paper and continue!

What do you think the impact is of the majority of psychological journals not including people of color as authors or as subjects in their studies?

How does the omission of people of color in research make you feel?

Do you think the Black male students you know feel that they can achieve anything they put their mind to?

How does your answer make you feel?

What are your most important takeaways from this chapter?

Prolepsis

Imagine that it's twenty years in the future. Every Black male student in your circle went to an Ivy League school, an HBCU, became an entrepreneur, or was successful in some manner. What did it take to make all the Black males in your circle college and career ready? What was your plan to make it happen?

Chapter 4

Understanding Issues Related to Black Male Health

It's the quality of life that matters, not the quantity.

—Dr. Llaila O Afrika (2016)

SANKOFA, THE IMPORTANCE OF LEARNING FROM THE PAST

Vignette

Father Love

A principal told me a story about a young Black male student who was always being sent to the nurse's office or always being referred to the social worker's office because of his classroom behavior. It happened so frequently that the principal decided to inquire more. The principal found out that the boy's mother and father divorced, and the father wasn't given joint custody. The student wasn't allowed to see his father. The principal contacted both of the parents and arranged for the father to call his son on designated days. On those days, the principal would let the student use the phone in his office. The Black male student's classroom behavior problems decreased. Students may have mental health issues related to things that even they don't understand. Unfortunately, behaviors that manifest as sadness—that is, being despondent, not talking, not looking a teacher in the eye, and having your head down— can be seen as a form of anger, disrespect, or insubordination and often leads to Black students being sent to the office and their subsequent expulsion.

In the last chapter, we discussed how a good outlook on life and a positive view of oneself leads to better academic outcomes. It stands to reason to think that negative thinking about life and oneself can have bad outcomes. The short answer is yes. For Black males, chances for positive outcomes seem so bleak they often become depressed. A guiding question for this chapter is: *How do we prepare Black males to successfully deal with life's challenges and plan strategies to navigate success?*

DEPRESSION

To begin, it is important to know that many Black males see depression as a form of weakness and therefore evade or ignore medical perspectives that would lead doctors to recognizing it as depression (Chapel, 2014). Additionally, the relationship to depression and district of social systems like health care and schooling are not favorable to Black males. For example, the symptoms and warning signs of adolescent and teen depression—poor concentration, moodiness, lack of motivation, disengagement from school, feeling misunderstood, a drop in grades, and failure to complete homework—are the same labels that are often attributed to Black males placed in special education programs and detention (Pediatrics, 2021). These frequently subjective warnings of depression create obstacles for Black boys that can lead to further impediments that may follow them for the rest of their lives. For example, Black male "push outs" from school (when students are encouraged to leave school for both legal and nonlegal reasons) are typically not because of violence or impaired intelligence but because of subjectively assessed behavioral norms that are often culturally biased. The overrepresentation of Black student suspension can start as early as preschool (Office for Civil Rights, 2015; CBS, 2014). Many feel that the psychological reaction to cyclical and repeated oppression that is often represented in schooling is a result of historical racial memory.

INTERNALIZED RACISM

While not directly related to depression, emotions such as anger and sadness toward racism can be internalized and lead to depression. When negative depictions and expectations related to race are so prevalent, they become normalized perceptions and behaviors and can be called internalized racism. There are at least three types of racism: mediated, institutionalized, and internalized (Jones, 2000). Looking at African American males between the ages of fourteen and nineteen in a Philadelphia high school, an African-centered charter high school, a youth detention facility, and a program that serves youth who are on probation or parole, Riccio, Hewlett, and Blake (2011) discovered that internalized racism explained 6 percent more variance in aggressive behavior, 3 percent more variance in attitudes toward guns and violence (Bryant, 2011), and 7 percent more variance in the overall propensity for violence (p. 703). Willis, Sosoo, Bernard, Neal, and Neblett (2021) assert that internalized racism can be linked to distress. The substantive message here is that internalized racism is an actual term that can be used to understand systematic and generational racism. Racism produces intergenerationally transmitted trauma (Henkeman, 2016).

POSTTRAUMATIC SLAVE SYNDROME

Coined by Joy DeGruy (2005), posttraumatic slave syndrome (PTSS) is a theory used to explain negatively adaptive survival strategies of multigenerational African descendants of enslavement. DeGruy (2005) asserts multigenerational trauma related to slavery, together with continued oppression, created the absence of opportunity to heal or to access true freedom, which in turn created PTSS. PTSS is characterized by a propensity for anger and violence, extreme feelings of suspicion, helplessness, literacy deprivation, and a distorted self-concept (DeGruy, 2005). Shari Hicks expands on DeGruy's research by recommending that those who caused PTSS should be studied more in depth than the victims of it.

The impacts of slavery affect Black people and especially Black male health outcomes related to depression and suspensions. However, other obstacles not related to depression are also found in the health care system.

HEALTH CARE INEQUITY

In the medical community, Black Americans are consistently undertreated for pain because of biased perceptions of Blacks having a higher tolerance for pain (Hoetetter & Klein, 2021). Specifically related to Black children, in 2017, Black children were five times more likely to be admitted to the hospital for asthma (US Department of Health and Human Services, 2021). Black children also have higher odds of death after surgery, higher odds of developing complications after surgery, and higher odds of serious adverse events, including cardiac arrest, sepsis, readmission, or reoperation after surgery, as well as higher mortality rates and are also more likely to be born with a lower birth weight (Nafiu et al., 2020; Effiong, Hogan, & Obasi, 2020).

The cumulative effects of health care inequity have a historical base that resounds in the Black community today. Many older generations of African American men are keenly aware of the Study of Untreated Syphilis in the Male Negro, better known as the Tuskegee Experiment, and elders' memories and opinions about this have led to younger generations of African American men being more likely to believe that Blacks are the targets of medical and scientific experiments. In 1933, hundreds of Black men in Tuskegee, Alabama, were intentionally and without their permission infected with syphilis and then denied treatment in an experiment to test the progression of the disease (Brandt, 1978). Unaware they had been infected with syphilis, they unknowingly spread the disease after sexual contact with wives and girlfriends. Therefore it affected not only them but also their families. This supports the reasoning behind the current generation of African Americans being more likely to believe that AIDS was created to destroy Blacks based on a previous historical precedent (Hoetetter & Klein, 2021).

RACE AND HEALTH

Black males are more likely to die from chronic diseases such as cardiovascular disease, diabetes, and cancer than White males and consequently have a lower life expectancy (Anderson, 2021). Poor health outcomes for Black males are found in all levels of education. The fact that all Black males are impacted by poor health despite educational level is surprising considering that the higher the educational attainment, the lower the life expectancy (Klisz-Hulbert, 2020). Also counterintuitive is the fact that the higher the educational attainment of Black males, the higher the depression rate (Klisz-Hulbert, 2020). Isolation, fewer social safety nets, and the fact that Black male professionals are less likely to have mentors all contribute to mental health pressures related to racism that are reflected in poor health outcomes.

For adolescent Black males, the social stigma of going to a psychiatrist, parent reluctance to having their child stigmatized as crazy, and teachers who are less likely to identify and encourage Black students to seek psychiatric care all contribute to the mental health issues of Black males (Alegría et al., 2012). Additionally, Black adolescents cite verbal abuse, differences from other people, and family problems as factors contributing to depression (Hannor-Walker et al., 2020). Part of the reason teachers are less likely to identify Black male depression is that Black boys as early as kindergarten are more likely to be seen as older and physically more mature, causing misperceptions of what depression may look like for Black male students (Hunt & Robles, 2018). Unfortunately, Black males psychological issues have not decreased resulting in the increase of suicide attempts as well as increased injury by suicide. Black male High school student suicide attempts increased between 1997 and 2017 (Lindsey, Sheftall, Xiao, & MPhil, 2019).

Suggestions to support mental health for Black male students include actively building trust by working collaboratively with social support networks, asking Black males directly about their negative experiences, incorporating aspects of Black spirituality, including outcome-based and goal-oriented clinical behavioral strategies, a thorough examination of negative attitudes toward taking medications, and self-exploration of biases of those who work with Black males as well as acknowledging their mistakes (Hankerson, Suite, & Bailey, 2015). Hannor-Walker, Bohecker, Ricks, and Kitchens (2020) suggest reducing stigmas associated with mental health therapy including increasing cultural education, while Anderson (2021) recommends culturally appropriate curriculum supporting Black student self-image and social relationships.

Mcintosh, Davis, Garraway, and Burt (2018) share that it is important to realize that when it comes to Black male issues related to their educational outcomes and mental health, educational policies like Every Student Succeeds Act were

> never designed to provide Black male students with an education that would (a) allow them to infringe on the White monopoly of intellectual, material, physical, and fiscal resources, (b) improve the lived realities of the masses of Black people, and (c) allow them to be self-sufficient. ESSA was designed and intended to ensure that Black male students could change their social conditions only through an education aligned to a White standard that would not threaten Whites' intellectual, social, and economic interests. (Mcintosh et al., 2018, p. 120)

In understanding issues related to Black male health, this chapter has shown that the struggle with Black male depression and inequitable health care is real. Some of the very things that define what a Black male is make him less likely to seek help. Black males, like all of us, need encouragement during difficult times in their lives. One way to support Black males is with affirming thoughts and behaviors. Hearing positive words tends to assuredly influence positive actions that all start with knowing the right words to say. Chapter 5 provides a few suggestions about positive terms to use with Black males.

CHAPTER 4 REFLECTION

Understanding Issues Related to Black Male Health

Guiding Question: How do we prepare Black males to successfully deal with life's challenges and plan strategies to navigate success?

In a relaxed and comfortable place, free write your answers to each of the questions for at least five minutes without concern for grammar or punctuation. If you need more room, just find another piece of paper and continue!

What do you think the impact of racism is on Black male students?

How does racism directed toward Black male students make you feel?

In what way does racism directed toward Black male students impact those around them?

How does dealing with racism directed toward Black male students and those around them make you feel?

What are your most important takeaways from this chapter?

Prolepsis

Imagine that you step into a classroom tomorrow morning. A Black male student is clearly upset over being called the "N" word. What method do you have to recognize depression in Black males, and what strategy or resources do you have to support him?

Chapter 5

Important Terms to Know When Working with Black Males

 Our failure to engage in this most important dialogue about race, racism, power . . . significantly limits the manner in which various individuals can talk about their experiences [and] also prevents us from hearing and empathizing with the pain, frustration, and deep-seated anger . . . particularly our young people, because they have been told that race is unimportant.

—Tyrone Howard (2008)

WOFORO DUA PA, SUPPORT, COOPERATION, AND ENCOURAGEMENT

Vignette

Black but Not American

My dad was in the air force, so we moved around a lot. One of the first places we moved to was a small town called Lakenheath in the United Kingdom. When we arrived in Lakenheath, I had just learned how to ride a bike. I remember struggling to keep myself from falling over and not running into anyone while riding around a small circular park near our house. I kept telling myself, "Don't hit the fence! Don't hit the fence!" So, of course, I wound up hitting the fence. And not one time but over and over again. I didn't notice it at first (it was all I could do to focus on keeping my bike upright), but I kept hearing the word "Yankee" every time I went around the park. Sometimes I heard the words "Damn Yankee." I soon realized that they were talking to me.

So I stopped my bike and got off (I basically just fell off), and I said, "Hey, I'm not a Yankee, I'm Black!" I didn't even know what being a Yankee meant. Over time, I came to learn that in the United Kingdom, I was thought of as an American—that is, a Yankee. All of my life up to that point, I had lived on the South Side of Chicago. In the United States I was just Black. No one had ever called me an American. And so my thoughts now are, "What would happen if all Black boys had an opportunity to be an American and not Black just for a little while?" "How much would they achieve?"

One of the most challenging questions we all ask ourselves is: *What do I say in this situation?* We often know what we want to say, but we search for the right language to use at the right times. This chapter highlights conceptual words and the thinking behind them so that the words we employ can be used as tools to positively communicate our thinking in an affirming way. A guiding question for this chapter is: *We often tell Black males we are here for them and support them, but how often do our words reflect our actions?*

Dr. Molife Asante asserts that "there can be no freedom until there is freedom of the mind. The first rule for freedom of the mind is the freedom of language" (2003, p. 41). Language, as Du Bois pointed out, can inform how we consciously observe and interact with the world (Du Bois, 1903). Language can also be viewed as a form of social capital. There are many forms of capital. To name just a few, there is teaching capital, the educational level, expertise, and time spent in the classroom of the teacher. Human capital is measured by professional knowledge and skills that are typically reflected in the level of education (Sullivan & Sheffrin, 2003). Cultural capital includes cultural habits and dispositions inherited from a family that is fundamental in school success (Bourdieu & Passeron, 1979).

Slightly related but different from cultural capital, social capital consists of networks and connections or "the ability of actors to secure benefits by virtue of membership in social networks or other social structures" (Portes, 1998, p. 6) that can be transmitted to children (Bourdieu, 1986). Social capital includes the actual or potential resources derived from investing in networks and relationship strategies, such as being involved in the community, making connections in the workplace, or being involved in clubs or organizations. Sometimes consciously or unconsciously, social capital requires investment in time to have both knowledge of and the ability to create occasions, places, and practices (such as cultural ceremonies) and skill at using them to maximum benefit (Bourdieu, 1986). However, not all Americans share capital equally.

AFFIRMATIVE ACTION

The term "affirmative action" was first used by President John F. Kennedy on March 6, 1961, when he issued Executive Order 10925, which mandated the following: "Take affirmative action to ensure that applicants are employed, and employees are treated during employment, without regard to their race, creed, color, or national origin." On September 24, 1965, President Lyndon B. Johnson issued Executive Order 11246, which prohibited employment discrimination based on race, color, religion, and national origin (and later in 1967 amended to include sex) by those organizations receiving federal contracts and subcontracts. President Johnson amended the order to include a person's gender on the list of attributes. It is important to note that while efforts have been made to reduce discrimination in the United States, prevalent and persistent fear toward the race and gender of Black males has not diminished.

AFROPHOBIA

"Afrophobia" (European Network Against Racism, 2014) is a term that refers to specific racism toward people of African and Afro-Latino descent that includes negative attitudes and feelings. Like anti-Semitism, in that anti-Semitism refers to how racism is enacted on people of Jewish descent, Afrophobia is observable discrimination against persons based on skin color, hair, ethnic origin, and nationality that has been statistically proven to be directed toward people of African descent economically, physically, psychologically, and biologically around the globe. Fear of people who look other than the accepted dominant culture has caused discrimination not only in the United States but also around the world.

DISCRIMINATION

The United Nations defines discrimination as

> any distinction, exclusion, restriction or preference based on race, colour, descent, or national or ethnic origin which has the purpose or effect of nullifying or impairing the recognition, enjoyment or exercise, on an equal footing, of human rights and fundamental freedoms in the political, economic, social, cultural or any other field of public life. (Office of the High Commissioner, Article 1, 1965)

Sonia Neito asserts this definition may be helpful conceptually but fails to describe the effects of discrimination and does not include a perspective that moves beyond looking at an entire group as representative of an individual (Neito, 2004).

REVERSE DISCRIMINATION

The premise of affirmative action is that it protected minorities from being exploited based on race, age, sexuality, creed, or nationality. When minorities are seen to have advantages or privileges that Whites do not, some call it reverse discrimination. Reverse discrimination is a phrase often used to describe a rare situation when women are perceived to be hired over White males just because they are women or when Black students are admitted to colleges over White candidates just because they are Black. The implication is that reverse discrimination occurs when minorities receive unfair advantages that negatively affect Whites. In other words, many bought into the idea that affirmative action would be free of bias and level the playing field equally for everyone, and because affirmative action did not mean that everyone was hired equally or at equal rates, it unfairly targeted benevolent Whites who tried to do good. However, reverse discrimination by its very definition, to separate or make distinct, would mean no discrimination. In other words, the opposite or the reverse of discrimination would be no discrimination regardless of a person's identity.

ETHNICITY

Ethnicity is defined as a microcultural group or collectivity that shares a common history, culture, values, behaviors, and other characteristics that cause members of the group to have a shared identity. "Ethnic groups share a sense of peoplehood and economic and political interests and are not the same as a racial group" (Banks & Banks, 2004, p. 445). However, people who belong to ethnic groups are often victims of housing discrimination from structural violence, redlining, segregation, and predatory lending because their ethnicity is perceived as a threat to the dominant social order.

STRUCTURAL VIOLENCE

Structural violence is defined as violence that kills slowly, such as the reduced opportunity for appropriate living conditions, unemployment and underemployment, and generational substandard schooling (Galtung & Höivik, 1971). Green describes structural violence when "class or race can be used to differentiate the length of an individual's life expectancy; this is an experience of violence without a direct actor to blame for it . . . it is built into social structures and institutions that are necessary and affect individual lives. Galtung also refers to structural violence as injustice and a form of inequity that can be measured by the distribution of power and its effects on individuals' lives" (Green, 2018, p. 4). Structural violence can also come in the form of restricting the movement of Black families from moving into White neighborhoods that can include physical barriers and sometimes metaphorically with visual information that represents physical barriers.

REDLINING

"Redlining was the practice of outlining areas with sizable Black populations in red ink on maps as a warning to mortgage lenders, effectively isolating Black people in areas that would suffer lower levels of investment than their white counterparts" (Perry & Harshbarger, 2019). Redlining includes both real estate agents and mortgage companies that steer racial minorities, primarily African Americans, into racially segregated communities (Kuebler & Rugh, 2013). One of the most egregious examples of redlining in New York was by the famous city designer Robert Moses who often constructed passageways to discourage minorities and the poor from having access to White neighborhoods including building bridges too low for buses and large trucks that nonwhites were more likely to use to travel (Campanella, 2017). Additionally, Moses destroyed thousands of houses of minority working-class people to build freeways through their own neighborhoods, crippling their communities and leading to the social stigma that Black neighborhoods were dirty and noisy. Even today, the social stigma associating Black communities as bad neighborhoods still exists. The demise and neglect of Black neighborhoods can be traced to both segregation and redlining as well as predatory lending.

SEGREGATION AND PREDATORY LENDING

Segregation and predatory lending are interrelated in at least four ways: "First, in segregated cities, minority communities are more isolated and maybe less experienced with purchasing financial products; second, mainstream prime lenders might avoid segregated, low-income areas; third, subprime lenders might target segregated areas with marketing strategies, exploiting and amplifying differences in financial education levels and the lack of access to prime lenders; and fourth, lenders may place a higher risk-based premium for those living in low- and moderate-income, segregated areas" (Dereck, Hyra, Squires, Renner, & Kirk, 2013, p. 178). In short, the homes the families of many Black males come from are likely to have been impacted by unfair housing policies.

For example, in the 1940s and 1950s the Federal Housing Authority (FHA) guaranteed bank loans for construction and development in the American North, the West, and Midwest under the condition that homes will not be sold to African Americans. Homeownership was a boon to the United States because there was a housing shortage after World War II (Shapiro, 2017). Additionally, Black neighborhoods were zoned for industrial plants and waste disposal sites that were kept out of White communities. That is one reason why Black neighborhoods became associated with slums. Although the Fair Housing Act was passed in 1968, it was too late for Black families who built homes before then. The homes built under racialized FHA policies were sold for an affordable $8,000 (about $100,000 in today's money). Today, those same homes sell for $300,000 to $400,000, while Blacks who lived in apartment buildings were not allowed to move into the suburbs.

RACIAL THREAT

Eitle, D'Alessio, and Stolzenberg (2002) assert that racial threat theory can effectively be used to examine how Whites, the dominant power group, use their disproportionate power to control minorities (read: subordinate groups) through social control. According to racial threat theory, there are at least three forms of racial threat: (1) economic, (2) political, and (3) symbolic (Blalock, 1967). It is the term "symbolic" that is particularly salient in *Mindful Teaching Practices for Black Male Achievement*. When minority groups like African Americans become more visible in White communities, coercive social control becomes more vehemently enforced (Arvanites, 2013). These forms of social control can take the form of increased detention/suspensions of Black males as well as punitive police stops. Quillian and Devah (2001) assert that fear of crime is higher in areas with majority populations of Blacks. Consequently, the higher the percentage of Black males in a community, the greater the perception of crime in the neighborhood (Quillian & Devah, 2001). "In a race-conscious society, an increasing African-American population in White areas may accentuate a sense of racial threat" (Arvanites, 2013, p. 436). It is not unreasonable to assume the increase of housing integration after the civil rights movement and the increase of African Americans in prisons or being shot by police officers is directly related to the racial threat.

ENDEARING TERMS TO USE WITH BLACK MALES

Words can both motivate as well as hinder self-perceptions and positive outcomes. Here is a list of words that can help Black males feel valued. These terms also have the benefit of shaping the language of positive group mindsets when used in meetings, proposals, and mission statements.

Adaptive
Bright
Collaborative
Communal
Communicative
Cool
Creative
Critical thinkers
Culturally rich
Diverse
Efficacious
Empowered
Enabled
Engaged
Enthusiastic
Excellent
Focused
Gifted
Hard working
High achieving
Intellectually curious
Proficient
Resilient
Responsible
Rewarding
Well-behaved
Young men of promise

Thus, so far, we have covered many topics that influence Black male success: social factors that affect education, social issues that affect educational outcomes, positive thinking, Black male depression, and affirming terms. But how do we use this information to increase success for Black males in the classroom? Chapter 6 answers that question and offers some advice.

CHAPTER 5 REFLECTION

Important Terms to Know When Working with Black Males Reflection

Guiding Question: *We often tell Black males we like and care about them as well as support them, but how often do our words and actions reflect our intent?*

In a relaxed and comfortable place, free write your answers to each of the questions for at least five minutes without concern for grammar or punctuation. If you need more room, just find another piece of paper and continue!

Do you think that Black male students believe that the world cares about them or their families?

How does your answer about Black male students and support or lack of support make you feel?

Do you think educators use the right language and supportive tone with Black male students?

How does your answer about language and tone used with Black male students make you feel?

What are your most important takeaways from this chapter?

Prolepsis

What does the future look like in a world where Black male students feel and are treated as if they were loved? What was your plan that made a supportive world for Black males?

Chapter 6

Recommendations and Conclusions for Black Male Success in the Classroom

 But that's just good teaching!

—Gloria Ladson-Billings (1994)

AKOMA, PATIENCE, AND TOLERANCE

Vignette

Playing through until the End

If you ever had a Black male in your classroom who never seems to listen, never seems to be paying attention, and you just couldn't make any connections with, and you secretly feel that he will never go anywhere in life, that same Black male was me at one time! Even today, when I look in the mirror, I don't see a reflection that looks like the teachers I've had in my life! I often did not connect with my teachers, nor did many of my teachers believe in me. My high school counselor actually told me that there was no need for me to take college prep classes. I got here frankly because I had a mother pray for me when it didn't even make sense. I never had any academic awards until the second year of my PhD program. But my mom being a patient mom said, "Well, if you are going to get an academic award, it's a pretty good idea to get one in a PhD program." I felt bad about that. During my K–12 experience, I was suspended so frequently and my mom had to come to school so often that she had her own parking spot with her name on it. But I eventually made it all the way to a PhD. Also, during my PhD program, I was a graduate teaching assistant. Things went fairly well for me in my PhD program. But in the very last semester of my PhD program, two things happened. One, my final graduate assistant check was delayed, and two, my travel reimbursement check for a conference that I attended was also delayed. I needed to have my graduation regalia (doctoral robes) for the graduation ceremony. But I did not have the money to pay for them. My mom offered to pay for them as a graduation present, but I said, "No, no! I can pay for it. I just need a loan until my checks come through." So she put my graduation regalia on her credit card. My regalia came in the mail three days before graduation! But they put the wrong color on my graduation hood. I scraped up the little money that I had, found a few yards of felt that was the right color, and found a tailor to fix my hood. It was finished at 5:00 p.m. the day before graduation. The funny part of the story is the university switched to a new robe design, and graduation was the first time anyone had seen the new robes. So while I was walking down the aisle with my new robe fixed just the day before, the president of the university had me stand up in front of everybody in attendance in the graduation audience, and he said, "Hey don't our new robes look sharp?" in front of the entire audience and graduating class. My mom got that on camera. My PhD graduation was the first time in my life where my mom had a chance to be proud of me in front of an audience, and it was literally the last few seconds left before I graduated with a doctorate. So the moral of this story is that you should never give up on a Black male student because he can come through even at the last minute. *True story!*

If you have noticed, there has not been much saying how the race of a teacher alone can positively or negatively affect educational outcomes of Black male students. All good teachers have the ability to effectively educate Black males regardless of race—it just takes good teaching. A guiding question for this chapter is: *What does good teaching for Black males look like in the classroom?*

Schools where Black male students are successful have educators that understand *social factors that influence educational outcomes*, including understanding male learning styles, work to dispel negative perceptions of Black males, and encourage positive individual and collective academic identities. In addition, successful schools for Black male students bridge obstacles to opportunities and consciously protect Black males from zero-tolerance policies and curricula that push them out of schools through *policies that foster positive educational outcomes*. Black male students are successful in classrooms that affirm and support their cultural and ethnic identities through *positive thinking that impacts perception and performance*. Educators who successfully teach Black male students *understand health issues related to Black males* that may affect educational outcomes and take ownership of knowing which *terms* to know and use *when working with Black males* for the best results. Some of the successful strategies that good teachers use and exemplify good teaching include the following.

PERSONAL GOAL SETTING

The most promising intervention for increasing minority male achievement is personal goal-setting techniques (Morisano, 2010). One study that examined the effects of personal goal setting found that, after the first year of the intervention, the male/female college graduation gap closed by 98 percent. Furthermore, the ethnicity gap closed by 38 percent and 93 percent in the second year (Schippers, Scheepers, & Peterson, 2015). Personal goal setting helps increase motivation and improves academic achievement because the participants articulate their own goals based on their own lived experiences. In addition, self-articulated goals are the most effective because they are self-directed. Overall, the results indicate that structured personal goal setting reduces male and ethnic minority inequalities.

STUDENT VOICE

Student voice is a strategy that engages youth in sharing their views on their experiences to make a meaningful change (Shapiro & Gross, 2013). When students are given opportunities to have meaningful conversations with their teachers and teachers turn that positive energy into motivation and encouragement, student voice can be a powerful source of transformational teacher change. In other words, students can provide invaluable information to teachers when they have the chance to be heard. Benner, Brown, and Jeffery (2019) have summarized a spectrum of student voice into six categories: (1) expression, (2) consolation, (3) participation, (4) partnership, (5) activism, and (6) leadership.

FEEDBACK

The ability to receive and ask for feedback is one of the best practices students can use to succeed academically (Hattie, 2012). Feedback is especially effective for students who have a positive view of constructive feedback and see feedback as an opportunity to improve through guided support. According to Yeager et al. (2014), students who were given critical feedback on essays from their teachers were better able to meet teacher standards. In addition, feedback can improve a student's likelihood of submitting revisions and improving the quality of final drafts. Positive effects of feedback were the strongest for African American students who previously felt distrust toward school (Yeager et al., 2014).

TEACHER INTERVENTION: POSITIVE PHONE CALLS HOME

The Michigan Department of Education has found an intervention called Positive Phone Calls Home to be an effective way to support Black male educational outcomes. Positive Phone Calls Home can transform parent-teacher conversations into positive engagements. The steps of Steps for Positive Phone Calls Home include the following:

> Establish a weekly schedule when you will make positive calls home so parents will know to expect your call.
>
> Begin the phone call by telling the parents you have some good news to share about their child so they aren't inclined to hang up because they are expecting a negative call.
>
> To the degree possible, try to avoid critical calls altogether because they send the implicit message that you as the teacher are having difficulty resolving the issue in your class independently. Frequent critical calls may also be perceived as you have a negative attitude toward African American male students.
>
> Be specific about what you observed and then describe what you see as the benefits the student is experiencing as the result of what the student is doing.

Be respectful and professional by showing appreciation for the parent's contribution and the complexity of raising a child. If a parent or guardian asks, be prepared to share ways they can support the positive behaviors at home.

Remember that these calls will, in many ways, define how the parent views you and the school (Shindler, 2009; Marshall, 2009).

EQUITY ETHIC

The Equity Ethics framework was created by McGee and Bentley (2017) to increase the number of students of color in science, technology, engineering, and mathematics (STEM) fields. The main idea behind the Equity Ethic is to switch the focus of STEM fields as lucrative nonaffirming jobs into opportunities to support and connect with the community. Naphan-Kingery et al.(2019) suggests that teachers can capitalize on the need for social justice practices in STEM fields by highlighting that students of color are more interested in helping their communities than working in White corporate America, where there is a prevalent lack of diversity. An Equity Ethics framework takes advantage of minority students' sense of value for social justice, empathy, and equity to help people as a means to recruit more underrepresented groups (McGee & Bentley, 2017). In other words, many Black male students do not necessarily need to see it to be it. Black male students are often motivated to increase racial and ethnic diversity in STEM fields when they see a lack of representation (McGee & Bentley, 2017).

CRITICAL RACE THEORY

Initially conceived by Derrick Bell, Critical Race Theory (CRT) grew out of legal studies and is used as a lens to examine the racial impact of legal actions. Ladson-Billings and Tate (1995) introduced the idea of utilizing CRT to understand the legal implications of education actions, such as *Brown v. Board of Education*, that segregated schools. Ladson-Billings and Tate (1995) assert that CRT is appropriate to examine inequalities in education because (1) race continues to be significant in the United States, (2) US society is based on property rights rather than human rights, and (3) the intersection of race and property creates an analytical tool for understanding inequity (p. 47). CRT shifts away from perspectives that suggest communities of color are culturally deficient (Yosso, 2005) and operates under the premise that Black students do not need to be rescued but need to be empowered. CRT is also employed by educators as a framework to analyze issues related to the educational system, the juvenile justice system, and barriers to Black male student success.

DISCOURSE DISCIPLINE

Discourse discipline is reading instruction based on the premise that every discipline has its own unique language and ways of using text to communicate information. Consequently, every discipline requires slightly different reading strategies to understand the content. While it may seem obvious as an adult, younger students who switch from having one teacher who teaches all of the topics often struggle with multiple topics taught by different teachers. However, the obstacles to learning during transitions are often not teacher related but learning strategy related. For example, the goals for reading math textbooks are to arrive at the "truth" or just one answer. The goals for reading chemistry textbooks require understanding the scientific process and paying close attention to corroboration and transformation. Reading history textbooks requires understanding the bias and perspective of the author, and often more than one source of information is required to see the entire picture. Understanding discourse discipline is important in high school as well as in college where philosophy textbooks focus on understanding the argument and do not focus on just one answer. Anthropology views fertility as the number of children a woman is capable of having, while in the medical field the definition of fertile means the number of children a woman actually conceives (Shanahan, Shanahan, & Misischia, 2011). Helping Black male students recognize different reading approaches and implement the right reading strategies can improve academic performance.

ETHNOMATHEMATICS

Ethnography combines the study of a living culture and the study of numbers, shapes, and patterns—that is, mathematics. Ethnomathematics challenges "the exchange of knowledge and power not just in the form of who teaches it and how but in the presentation of *who* has the *right* to learn such behavior" (Nicholson, 1968, p. 33). Many Indigenous cultures' use of mathematics in astronomy and medicine was not valued because they were not viewed as math or science.

For example, Professor Ron Englash asserts in his book *African Fractals: Modern Computing and Indigenous Design* (2005) that there is intentional complex mathematics in Indigenous African designs that often go unnoticed. From village construction design to clothing, Africans have historically and consistently used geometric algorithms, complex numeric systems, recursions, and fractal geometry throughout history. Fractals are infinitely complex neverending patterns that are self-similar across different scales in an ongoing feedback loop (Mandelbrot, 1977). Ethnomathematics is incredibly empowering and affirming to members of cultures that have been unfairly viewed as mathematically and intellectually "nonliterate" (Ascher & Ascher, 1997). Many African cultures have sophisticated mathematic equations etched in stone artifacts, clay masks, and cloth that are viewed merely as simple art and not knowledge of mathematics. Two examples of undervalued mathematics of African culture include Kente cloth (colorful mathematic patterns that represent a pattern like 0s and 1s in computer language) and hieroglyphics (patterns and designs that depict images as well as numbers) (Ransaw, 2012; Browder, 1992).

Black males have been portrayed as *less than*. Black males have been depicted in early forms of media such as paintings and posters as less than human, less than intelligent, less than worthy of respect, and less than cultur-ally adaptable. Today, Black males are depicted in modern forms of media such as broadcast news and the internet as sports figures, entertainers, and people who are prone to violence. Racial biases become beliefs and behav-iors and in turn become policies based on more deficit assumptions rather than viewing cultural differences as assets. Affecting everything from rapport to engagement, teachers who make heartfelt connections with Black males based on authentic and sincere intentions are the crucial element to Black males' success in school and in life.

A SPECIAL NOTE

In a book written mostly about Black males, it is all too easy to give the impression that multicultural points of view are not valued. This book implores educators, parents, and policymakers to support efforts that cultivate good relationships between Black boys and teachers early in their lives. However, all students should be valued in the classroom and in life. Preschool years are formative in helping all students, but especially Black male students, find their own self-identities and create strategies to connect with all their classmates. It is especially important to acknowledge that encouraging harmonious interac-tions between Black boys and teachers early in life can mitigate many issues that affect Black male/teacher relationships in the future.

CONCLUSION

Mindful Teaching Practices for Black Male Achievement highlighted a few topics to help think about improving Black male academic success and how to better address the bountiful opportunities that Black males can have. It is all too easy to exclude Black males as part of an ethnic problem instead of an American problem. Exclusionary attitudes toward Black males are reflec-tive of systematic educational, social, and employable disenfranchisement. Holding up a few Black males who have succeeded academically as authentic examples of what it means to be Black is disingenuous when many Black males are held back or pushed out of school. People remember Black males when they score for their favorite college or professional team but forget them after graduation and overlook them when it is time to look for employees.

However, there is hope. Black males are completing high school at a higher rate, graduating from colleges at increasingly higher rates, and are earning more than ever before in American history. While these triumphs are not without a great cost, they have made the journey more tolerable. "Human progress is neither automatic nor inevitable. . . . Every step toward the goal of justice requires sacrifice, suffering, and struggle; the tireless exertions and passionate concern of dedicated individuals," said Dr. King in his 1961 March on Washington speech (King, 2013). It is important to remember that education does not free Black males. Black males are already free. Black males do not need to be rescued. Black males need resources and support to excel, just as teachers need resources and support to succeed. This book is one step along the path of progress for Black males. However, the next step toward a great destiny begins with you. Please utilize the informative resources found in the Appendix of this book, which includes helpful websites, groups, and organizations as well as templates to write teachers and educators, police administrators, and state representatives to support Black male students.

CHAPTER 6 REFLECTION

Recommendations and Conclusions for Black Male Success in the Classroom

Guiding Question: *What does good teaching for Black males look like in the classroom?*

In a relaxed and comfortable place, free write your answers to each of the questions for at least five minutes without concern for grammar or punctuation. If you need more room, just find another piece of paper and continue!

In your mind, what do Black males think good teaching looks like in their classrooms?

How does your answer about Black male student perspective about good teaching make you feel about your own teaching practices?

What do *you* think good teaching looks like for Black male students?

How does *your* answer about what good teaching looks like for Black male students influence how you make connections with them?

What are your most important takeaways from this chapter?

Prolepsis

Imagine that the future was today. You have had positive relationships with all your Black male students for the past five years.

Now ask your future self:
What changed?
How did it happen?
What was your plan to get here?

Culminating Reflection

Congratulations! You've finished reading *Mindful Teaching Practices for Black Male Achievement*!

Please find a quiet place where you are relaxed.
Inhale deeply and exhale slowly three times.
Visualize your journey with *Mindful Teaching Practices for Black Male Achievement*.

Think again about the time when you had a relationship with a Black male that wasn't as fulfilling as you would have liked.

Free write your answers to each of the questions for at least twenty minutes without concern for grammar or punctuation. If you need more room, just find another piece of paper and continue!

What have you learned about yourself?
How has the thinking about your role interacting with Black male students changed?
How have your feelings about how to address meaningful relationships with Black male students changed?

After reading *Mindful Teaching Practices for Black Male Achievement* and looking over your reflections and prolepsis responses, in what way has the things that matter most in your life (family, friendships, career, etc.) been impacted?

After reading *Mindful Teaching Practices for Black Male Achievement* and looking over your reflections and prolepsis responses, in what way has your role as (an educator, a healer, an advisor, a mentor, a sister, a friend of a Black male, other) changed?

After reading *Mindful Teaching Practices for Black Male Achievement* and looking over your reflections and prolepsis responses, what is something new you would like Black male students to know about you?

After reading *Mindful Teaching Practices for Black Male Achievement* and looking over your reflections and prolepsis responses, what more would you like to know about Black males?

After reading *Mindful Teaching Practices for Black Male Achievement* and looking over your reflections and prolepsis responses, what do you think are some of the takeaways to develop meaningful relationships with Black male students?

After reading *Mindful Teaching Practices for Black Male Achievement* and looking over your reflections and prolepsis responses, how will you use the information to foster even better relationships with your Black male students?

Prolepsis

Imagine that two educators told you that they are from the future, and they were here to observe you because your actions today became the model of teaching not just for Black male students but for all the students on the planet. What will you do that will change the world?

Chapter 7

Mindful Teaching Practices for Black Male Achievement Toolkit

HWE MU DUA, MEASURING STICK

Historical Influences of Education Policy on African Americans

Theodore Ransaw, PhD

Background: If you cannot see a student, how can you teach him? Black males feel invisible in the classroom, only present as examples of what not to do, seen only when they do something wrong, and viewed as unable and uninterested in school, students who only want to play sports. The exclusion of Black males from almost everything positive in the American learning system is not just opinion; it is a statement of fact based on historical precedent. Based on inequitable suspensions and expulsions, as well as the prevalence of special education referrals, the American education system has taught Black males and teachers their individual and cultural makeups make them uneducable. Consequently, Black males often feel intellectually and emotionally abandoned by their teachers and schools. Unable to be truly educated in the United States for centuries from traditional curriculum, learning the null curriculum, schooling that entails decoding and interpreting cultural expectations outside of their experience has made it almost impossible for Black males to thrive. The null curriculum is what we teach by not teaching it (Harris, 1992; Kazemi et al., 2020).

Objectives: To build upon or increase student engagement in ways that affirm Black male identity.

Outcomes: To support positive Black male student and teacher relationships by providing teachers with background information about the historical influence of education policies of Blacks in America.

DIRECTIONS

1. Read the "Historical Influences of Education Policy on African Americans Timeline."
2. Reflect on the information and write down your thoughts.
3. Organize your thoughts and be mindful of how historic oppressive education legislation has impacted America today.

HISTORICAL INFLUENCES OF EDUCATION POLICY ON AFRICAN AMERICANS TIMELINE

1635—The first American public school is established in Boston.

1740—South Carolina outlaws education of Africans or employment of enslaved Africans as scribes.

1787—Northwest Ordinance divides the Michigan territory into townships. Taxes from these townships fund schools.

1823—Education of enslaved and free Africans is outlawed in Mississippi.

1828—First public school is established in Michigan.

1831—North Carolina and Virginia outlaw the teaching of enslaved Africans.

1831—North Carolina passes a bill forbidding a White man or woman from teaching a slave to read or write by fine or imprisonment. A slave who teaches another slave to read or write shall be sentenced to thirty-nine lashes.

1834—Prudence Crandall is placed in jail for educating Black girls in Canterbury, Connecticut.

1852—Frederick Douglass delivers his *What to a Slave* speech in Rochester, New York, highlighting discrepancies in the Declaration of Independence toward Negros.

1853—Margaret Douglass is jailed for teaching Blacks to read in Norfolk, Virginia.

1857—*Dred Scott v. Sandford* US Supreme Court case rules that people of African descent imported as slaves and their descendants—free or not—are not considered citizens of the United States.

1861—The American Civil War divides the states into Union North / free states and Confederate South / slave states.

1862—Emancipation Proclamation executive order is issued by President Lincoln: "All persons held as slaves within any State or designated part of a State, shall be then, thenceforward, and forever free."

1862—Morrill Lang Grants are created to establish land-grant colleges.

1865—Thirteenth Amendment to the Constitution: "Neither slavery nor involuntary servitude, except as a punishment for crime whereof the party shall have been duly convicted, shall exist within the United States, or any place subject to their jurisdiction."

1875—Kalamazoo, Michigan, establishes public high schools funded by taxes. Kalamazoo later uses the same ruling to establish a university and later the first agricultural college in America.

1876–1965 The Jim Crow Laws enforce racial separation between Whites and Blacks, including schools that were authorized by state and local governments.

1896—*Plessy v. Ferguson* US Supreme Court case rules that racial separation is illegal. This catapulted the phrase "separate but equal" based on the Thirteenth Amendment, which abolished slavery and involuntary servitude, *except as a punishment for crime.*

1899—W. E. B. Du Bois publishes *The Philadelphia Negro*, the first urban ethnography of African Americans.

1899—Booker T. Washington publishes *The Future of the American Negro*, which pushes the notion that African Americans, newly released from slavery, should focus on economic security and education.

1903—W. E. B. Du Bois publishes his views on *double consciousness*, the belief that African Americans may be able to look at their experiences with a "divided self" and to see the world through multiracial eyes—an intuitiveness that enables them to perceive society from a unique moral perspective.

1904—The Washington–Du Bois Conference of 1904 sets the stage for African American intellectual debate on issues of education.

1933—Carter G. Woodson publishes *The Mis-Education of the Negro*, which asserts that Eurocentric frames of thinking and valuing knowledge historically has neglected the contribution of people of African descent.

1944—The Servicemen's Readjustment Act, commonly known as the GI Bill, allows many African American servicemen to attend college and vocational schools after World War II.

1954—*Brown v. Board of Education of Topeka I* US Supreme Court case rules that separate but unequal education of Black and White children was unconstitutional. However, while not officially legal, education in the United States is still unofficially separate and unequal.

1955—*Brown v. Board of Education II*: The language "all deliberate speed." The US District Court rules that Prince Edward County, Virginia, did not have to desegregate immediately. White students in the county were given assistance to attend White-only "private academies" that were taught by teachers formerly employed by the public school system, while Black students had no education at all unless they moved out of the county.

1955—Little Rock Nine: Nine students are barred from integrating Little Rock Central High School by the Arkansas National Guard sent by Arkansas governor Orval Faubus. President Eisenhower sends the US Army's 101st Airborne Division to escort the Little Rock Nine to school and in classes for a year.

1964—The Civil Rights Act of 1964 extends the Civil Rights Act of 1875 to include outlawing public discrimination in public facilities including schools.

1965—Lyndon B. Johnson signs the Elementary and Secondary School Act into law emphasizing a war on poverty forbidding a national curriculum but encouraging equal access, high standards, and accountability.

1965—Daniel Patrick Moynihan publishes the Moynihan Report, also known as "The Negro Family: The Case for National Action." "America is free to chose whether the Negro shall remain her liability or become her opportunity."

1970—Paulo Freire publishes *Pedagogy of the Oppressed*, which suggests a removal of the idea of the banking system of education where teachers are merely depositors of information and suggests that teachers should embrace a facilitator model of education that values the culture and worldview of their students.

1970—Clifton Wharton is elected president of Michigan State University. Dr. Wharton was president at MSU for eight years and the first Black president of a major US university.

1971—William Cross publishes his *Nigrescence* (African American Identity Model), which he asserts occurs in four steps: (1) pre-encounter, (2) encounter, (3) immersion/emersion, and (4) internalization.

1975—Gregory Foucault publishes *Discipline and Punish*, which asserts that punishment becomes the model for control of an entire society including which are schools modeled on the prison system.

1976—Dr. Eric Bell publishes "Serving Two Masters: Integration Ideals and Client Interests in School Desegregation Litigation" in the *Yale Law Review*. Critical race theory (CRT) is born. A critical look at desegregation and bussing did little to improve the Black community.

1978—The *Brown v. Board of Education III* case is reopened, and the open enrollment for schools that had the potential to continue to divide Black and White school children is upheld.

1982—Zero tolerance ("Just say no."—Nancy Reagan): President Ronald Reagan declares the war on drugs, which starts the impetus for zero-tolerance policies for students who have drugs on campus.

1986—John Ogbu releases his burden of "acting white" theory. Ogbu asserted that both societal and school discrimination, instrumental community factors such as perceptions of lack of jobs, *and* Black oppositional culture are three interrelated factors in which to examine Black students' low academic behavior.

1988—Molefi Asante publishes *Afrocentricity*, which states that the heart of Afrika should be at the heart of everything you do including the welfare of all its people (and its students).

1989—The Drug-Free School and Campuses Act banned the unlawful use, possession, or distribution of drugs and alcohol by students and employees on school grounds and college campuses. This act prompted schools to enact severe disciplinary sanctions for student violations or risk losing federal aid.

1990—Janet Helms introduces her White Racial Identity Attitude Scale (WRIAS), which involves six sequential stages: (1) contact, (2) disintegration, (3) reintegration, (4) pseudo-independence, (5) immersion/emersion, and (6) autonomy.

1991—*Board of Education of Oklahoma City v. Dowell* rules that desegregation orders were temporary and sanctions a return to segregated neighborhood schools for districts that have made good faith efforts to desegregate and remedied past discrimination "as far as practicable."

1994—The Gun-Free School Act requires every state to pass a law requiring educational agencies to expel from school, for not less than one year, any student found in possession of a gun.

1995—Prison construction surpasses college construction for the first time.

1995—*Missouri v. Jenkins* rules that Kansas City's desegregation plan to lure suburban Whites to inner-city magnet schools was overambitious and overturned a lower court decision to maintain magnet schools.

2002—No Child Left Behind (George W. Bush) is signed into law emphasizing high standards including standards-based education.

2003—*Grutter v. Bollinger United States Supreme Court* upholds the affirmative action policy at the University of Michigan Law School.

2005—The American Psychological Association commissions a task force to examine zero-tolerance discipline policies in elementary and secondary education.

2005—Florida is the first state to approve the Stand Your Ground Law. Stand Your Ground gives individuals the right to use deadly force to defend themselves without having to retreat from a person who poses an immediate threat or who feels that they are in imminent danger.

2009—Race to the Top (Barack Obama): States are awarded incentives for meeting education policies that include performance-based and common core standards.

2011—Education secretary Arne Duncan and attorney general Eric Holder announce the launch of a collaborative project: the Supportive School Discipline Initiative between the US Departments of Education (ED) and Justice (DOJ) to support the use of school discipline practices that foster safe, supportive, and productive learning environments while keeping students in school.

2012—Michigan governor Rick Snyder and Michigan Department of Education superintendent Michael Flanagan announce a resolution to address school discipline issues impacting student outcomes.

2013—Trayvon Martin is shot to death by George Zimmerman while suspended from school.

2013—Congressional hearing about the school-to-prison pipeline is chaired by Senator Richard Durbin (D-IL).

REFERENCES

Bell, E. (1992). *Faces at the bottom of the well: The permanence of racism.* New York: Basic Books.

Black Past.org. (2014). *The Moynihan report (1965).* Retrieved from http://www .blackpast.org/primary/moynihan-report-1965#sthash.V5048wsv.dpuf.

Clark, C., Jenkins, M., and Stowers, G. P. (forthcoming). *Fear of da' gangsta': The social construction, production, and reproduction of violence in schools for corporate profit and the revolutionary promise of critical multicultural education.* Westport, CT: Greenwood.

Cross, William E. (1971). "The Negro-to-Black Conversion Experience." *Black World, 20*(9): 13–27.

City of Boston. (2014). *First public school site and Ben Franklin statue.* Retrieved from http://www.cityofboston.gov/freedomtrail/firstpublic.asp.

Davis, A. Y. (1997). Race and criminalization: Black Americans and the punishment industry. In R. Delgado and J. Stefancic (2001). *Critical race theory: An introduction.* New York: New York University Press.

Du Bois, W. E. B. (1899). *The Philadelphia Negro.* New York: Lippincott.

Emancipation Proclamation (1863/2013). Retrieved from http://www .emancipationproclamation.org.

Ferguson, A. (2001). *Bad boys: Public schools in the making of Black masculinity.* Ann Arbor: University of Michigan Press.

Freire, P. (2000). *Pedagogy of the oppressed.* New York: Continuum.

Hacker, A. (1992). *Two nations: black and white, separate, hostile, unequal.* New York: Ballantine Books.

Harris, M. D. (1992). Africentrism and curriculum: Concepts, issues, and prospects. *Journal of Negro Education, 61*, 301–16.

Harvard Civil Rights Project. (1999). Harvard Civil Rights Project Reports rise in school segregation. *Civil Rights Monitor, 10*(4). Retrieved from http://www .civilrights.org/monitor/fall1999/art6p1.html.

Kazemi, S., Ashraf, H., Motallebzadeh, K., and Zeraatpishe, M. (2020). Development and validation of a null curriculum questionnaire focusing on 21st century skills using the Rasch model. *Cogent Education, 7*(1), 1–17. DOI: 10.1080/2331186X.2020.1736849.

Lasswel, H. D. (1936). *Politics: Who gets what, when, how*. New York: McGraw-Hill.

Lawnix. (2014). *Plessy v. Ferguson—Case brief summary*. Retrieved from http:// www.lawnix.com/cases/plessy-ferguson.html.

Lubiano W. (Ed.). (1996). *The house that race built: Black Americans, U.S. terrain.* New York: Anchor.

Mimms, E. (2007). *Equity in K–12 public education.* Ann Arbor: University of Michigan School of Education. Retrieved from http://sitemaker.umich.edu/ educationalequity/african_american_timeline.

North Carolina General Assembly. (1830). *A bill to prevent all persons from teaching slaves to read or write, the use of figures excepted (1830)*. Legislative Papers, 1830–31 Session of the General Assembly. Retrieved from http://www.learnnc.org /lp/editions/nchist-newnation/4384.

Office of Superintendent of Public Instruction. (2013). *Elementary and Secondary School Act (ESEA)*. Washington, DC: Department of Education. Retrieved from http://www.k12.wa.us/ESEA/default.aspx.

Ogbu, J. (2003). *Black American students in an affluent suburb: A study of academic disengagement (sociocultural, political, and historical studies in education)*. New York: Routledge.

Ransaw, T. (2013). *The art of being cool: The pursuit of Black masculinity*. Chicago: African American Images.

Smith, B. (1965). *They closed their schools*. Chapel Hill: University of North Carolina Press.

US Department of Education. (2009). *Race to the top program executive summary*. Washington, DC: Department of Education.

US Department of Labor, Office of Policy Planning and Research. (1965). *The Negro family: The case for national action.* East Lansing: University of Michigan Library.

Washington, B. T. (2013). *The future of the American Negro*. Seattle: Creative Space Independent Publishing Platform.

Woodson, C. G. (1933/2009). *The mis-education of the Negro*. New York: Wilder Publications.

**Best Practices for Closing Black Male Student Achievement/
Opportunity Gaps by Grade Level**

Theodore S. Ransaw, PhD

Background: When Black male students fail, we all fail. If we fail to make connections with Black males, it is not because of their own doing but because we missed opportunities to help them achieve. The best practices here are a compilation of time-tested and research-based strategies as well as new and innovative ones (Tables 7.1–7.4). These suggestions may work for other age groups; however, these tips were placed into categories based on grade level.
Objectives: To build upon or increase Black male educational student success and career and college readiness.
Outcomes: To support positive Black male student and teacher relationships by providing a model of how to create and implement a behavioral observation intervention plan specifically tailored to their classroom.

DIRECTIONS

1. Read *Mindful Teaching Practices for Black Male Achievement.*
2. Look over the following example of a successful interaction between a Black male student and teacher.
3. Use the completed "Black Male Behavioral Intervention Plan" as a model to fill out your own blank "Black Male Behavioral Observation Intervention Plan" (see pages 69–70) using the information you have learned from *Mindful Teaching Practices for Black Male Achievement* and your idealized intended strategy and desired outcomes.

BEST PRACTICES

Table 7.1. Pre-K/K Best Practices

1	Remember that adopting new curricula does not, in general, produce large improvements in learning outcomes. Changing teaching practices, through extensive continuing professional development, is the most powerful classroom strategy for closing attainment gaps.
2	Structured phonics instruction, cooperative learning, frequent assessment, and teaching meta-cognitive skills (for example, "learning to learn") can significantly raise outcomes.
3	Structured phonics-based approaches, in general, work better than nonphonics approaches.
4	Offer reading circles and encourage working in smaller groups.
5	Provide parental material promoting parent advocacy and student nutrition.
6	Suggest parents ask their child three things they learned each day.

7	For parents who may be unable to listen to their children read before bedtime, suggest recording their kids' reading to monitor progress.
8	Encourage participation in PSAT.
9	Share best practices to other teachers in the school.
10	Financing teacher cultural awareness, African drumming, poetry, etc.

REFERENCES

C4EO. (2011). *Effective classroom strategies for closing the gap in educational achievement for children and young people living in poverty, including white working-class boys*. London: Centre for Excellence and Outcomes in Children and Young People's Services.

Cooper, E. J. (2005). It begins with belief: Social demography is not destiny. *Voices from the Middle, 13*(1), 25–33.

Epstein, J. (1995). School/family/community partnerships: Caring for the children we share. *Phi Delta Kappan, 76*(9), 701–12.

Flaxman, E. (2003). *Closing the achievement gap: Two views from current research.* Eric Digest ED482919. Retrieved April 6, 2012, from http://www.ericdigests.org /2004-3/gap.html.

Gibson, H. V. (2010). *Improving academic achievement for Black male students: Portraits of successful teachers' instructional approach and pedagogy.* Cambridge, MA: Harvard University Press.

Harris, M. D. (1992). Africentrism and curriculum: Concepts, issues, and prospects. *Journal of Negro Education, 61*, 301–16.

HB 2722 Advisory Committee. (2008). *A plan to close the achievement gap for African American Students. Olympia, WA: Office of Superintendent of Public Instruction. Retrieved April 6, 2013, from http://www.k12.wa.us/cisl/pubdocs/ AfrAmer%20AchGap%20Rpt%20FINAL.pdf.*

Henderson, A. T., and Mapp, K. L. (2002). *A new wave of evidence: The impact of school, family, and community connections on student achievement: Annual synthesis 2002.* Austin, TX: National Center for Family and Community Connections with Schools. Retrieved from http://ezproxy.msu.edu/login?url=http://search .proquest.com/docview/1312422437?accountid=12598.

Hu, H. (2007, April). To close gaps, schools focus on black boys. *New York Times.* Retrieved April 6, 2013, from http://www.nytimes.com/2007/04/09/nyregion /09school.html?pagewanted=all&_r=1&.

Irvine, J. (1990). *Black students and school failure.* Westport, CT: Greenwood.

Jackson, Y. (2011). *The pedagogy of confidence: Inspiring high intellectual performance in urban schools.* New York: New York Teachers College Press.

Jackson, Y., and McDermott, V. (2012). *Aim high achieve more: How to transform urban schools through fearless leadership.* Alexandria, VA: ACSD.

Johnson, J. (2013). *Closing the achievement gap in K–12.* Conducted at AdvancED/ MDE Spring School Improvement Conference. Lansing, MI: Lansing Conference Center.

Table 7.2. Elementary School Best Practices

1	Rigorous curriculum with strong emphasis on STEM areas and language development.
2	Expand mathematics, engineering, science applications (MESA) to the elementary level.
3	Seat those who are not performing as well closer to teachers.
4	Provide longer wait time for those not performing as well to answer.
5	Give those not performing as well clues or try repeating or rephrasing the question.
6	Do not criticize students who are not performing as well more often for failure.
7	Interact with students who are not performing as well more publicly than privately.
8	Décor of classroom should be inspirational and culturally reinforcing.
9	Implement a high level of self-respect for all students.
10	Provide equitable response opportunities for all students.
11	Maintain equitable feedback for all students.
12	Ensure that students ask more questions than the teacher.
13	Develop critical thinking skills by asking open-ended questions.
14	Implement assertive, consistent, complementary, and clearly established rules and consequences.
15	Provide cooperative learning experiences.
16	Create and enforce stipulations that if parents do not complete their school volunteer hours, their child's younger siblings will not be considered for admission.
17	Create a schoolwide atmosphere that encourages parental involvement.
18	Provide parent manuals with tips and guidelines.

Table 7.3. Middle School Best Practices

1	Assume parents care about their children and want the best for them.
2	Make positive calls to the student's home.
3	Provide student access to computers during lunch and after school hours.
4	Offer RTI/MTSS that supports students by utilizing the best subject matter teachers working with the students who need the most help.
5	Offer college and career readiness programs.
6	Dropout prevention and retrieval programs.
7	Provide rigorous curriculum with strong emphasis on STEM areas and language development.
8	Remember that parents may have had a bad experience in school that serves as a barrier to parental involvement.
9	Hold PTAs, PTOs, and CBOs in apartment complexes, community centers, and other faith-based institutions where parents feel safe.
10	Do not assume parents are literate in *any* language.
11	Remember that in elementary school parents have one teacher to talk to; middle school has more than one, which can be intimidating.
12	Have someone greet parents at the door during parent-teacher conferences to provide directions and a welcoming environment.
13	Facilitate parents reading and understanding school improvement plans.
14	Offer resume writing class, *not* parental education classes.

Table 7.4. High School Best Practices

1	Provide clear curriculum choices for students.
2	Offer both remediation and acceleration courses.
3	Facilitate wraparound student support.
4	Be responsible for providing easily accessible adult support.
5	Facilitate opportunities that involve the whole family.
6	Offer a clear and deep focus on college preparation.
7	Demystify the college-going experience for students and parents.
8	Articulate a transparent and outlined initiative of reforms, specifically targeting the persistence of an achievement gap.
9	Utilize frequent assessments of student progress and multiple opportunities for improvement.
10	Employ an emphasis on nonfiction writing.
11	Encourage collaborative scoring of student work.
12	Deliver a rigorous curriculum.
13	Provide a clear and deep focus on academic achievement.
14	Real-world experiences.
15	Reduce student-to-teacher ratio whenever you can.
16	Identify students who are not at proficiency based on NEAP and intervene early utilizing the subject matter teachers for classroom prep before class and/or after class.
17	Document by log which group/individual is helping which student so that all intervention is data driven.
18	Remember that student interest and homework completion wanes depending on the time of the school year.
19	Know where each and every student is in regard to GPA and classes they need to take to stay on track for graduation.
20	Empower principals to be instructional leaders.
21	Teach for mastery.
22	Encourage and support teacher collaboration.
23	Hire teachers that hold themselves accountable.
24	Utilize targeted professional development.
25	Create a climate where teachers value professional learning.
26	Employ continuous improvement strategies.
27	Make sound fiscal management.

Kunjufu, K. (2009). *How to improve the academic achievement in African American males. Recruitment resource center for prospective teachers.* Teachers of Color: Recruitment Resource Center for Prospective Teachers. Retrieved April 6, 2013, from http://www.teachersofcolor.com/2009/11/how-to-improve-academic-achievement-in-african-american-males/.

Lai, J., and Bishil, D. (2005). *A review of effective district practices used nationwide to close the achievement gap* (Los Angeles Unified School District Program Evaluation and Research Branch Planning, Assessment, and Research Division Report No. 263). Los Angeles, CA: LAUSD.

Lewis, S., Simon, C., Uzzell, R., Horwtiz, A., and Casserly, M. (2010). *A call for change: The social and educational factors contributing to the outcomes of Black males in urban schools.* Washington, DC: Council of Great City Schools.

Reeves, D. (2009). *Uncovering the "secrets" of high poverty, high success schools.* Teachers of Color: Recruitment Resource Center for Prospective Teachers. Retrieved April 6, 2012, from http://www.teachersofcolor.com/2009/04/uncovering -the-secrets-of-high-poverty-high-success-schools/.

Slavin, R. E., and Madden, N. A. (2006). Reducing the gap: Success for all and the achievement of African American students. *Journal of Negro Education, 75*(3), 389–400. Retrieved from http://ezproxy.msu.edu/login?url=http://search.proquest .com/docview/222071665?accountid=12598.

Urban Education Network of Iowa. (2003). *Strategies for closing the achievement gap.* Des Moines: Urban Education Network Iowa.

WestEd. (2006). *Charter high schools closing the achievement gap: Innovation in education.* Jessup, MD: ED Pubs, Education Publications Center, US Department of Education.

White, H. E. (2009, March). *Increasing the achievement of African American males* (Report from the Department of Research, Evaluation, and Assessment 3). Virginia Beach, VA: Department of Research, Evaluation, and Assessment. Retrieved April 6, 2013, from http://www.vbschools.com/accountability/research_briefs/ aamalebrieffinalamarch.pdf.

Woolley, M. E., and Grogan-Kaylor, A. (2006). Protective family factors in the context of neighborhood: Promoting positive school outcomes. *Family Relations, 55*, 95–106.

Behavioral Observation Intervention Plan

Theodore S. Ransaw, PhD

Background: Many interactional problems in the classroom are based on student comprehension issues and teacher frustration of expectation violations that may include a Black male student appearing to be disengaged in school or silent. However, Watzlawick's first axiom states that a person cannot not communicate (Watzlawick, Beavin Bavelas, & Jackson, 1967). In other words, everything we do communicates a message—whether we intend it to or not. Communication occurs even when we are silent. For students, silence can communicate disengagement from schooling, or it can express embarrassment from not understanding instruction. Both powerful and moving, silence can be just as effective as verbal expressions. Either way, whether verbal or nonverbal, we all communicate. So when a teacher says that a student "just sits there, with no communication whatsoever," the student *is*, in fact, communicating. By being aloof, detached, and silent, many Black males are engaging in a *cool pose* as a form of resistance to oppression (Majors & Billson, 1992). This silent stoicism has also been described as the *cool factor*: a behavior that Black males adopt to balance their social capital with their academic capital by not appearing too nerdy or too dumb—just cool (Ransaw, 2013). This cool behavior, which intersects race, class, and gender (Wilkins, 2008), is often adopted as a masculine shield against uncomfortable situations. Acting cool is an expressive form of cultural and gendered identity that is typically a nonverbal form of communication and can be misinterpreted because it does not conform with expectations. Expectation violations are misalignments between student and teacher interactions often based on misinterpreted cultural decoding of masculine behavior, including acting cool.

Outcomes: To support positive Black male student and teacher relationships by providing a model of how to create and implement a behavioral observation intervention plan specifically tailored to their classroom.

Description: Many behavioral interaction problems in the classroom are based on student comprehension issues and teacher frustration. Creative solutions often involve creating opportunities based on a student's strengths.

Objectives: To build upon or increase student comprehension in ways that affirm Black male identity.

DIRECTIONS

1. Read *Mindful Teaching Practices for Black Male Achievement.*
2. Look over the example of a successful interaction between a Black male student and teacher (Table 7.5).

Table 7.5. Behavioral Observation Intervention Plan

Observation: Very specific; who, what, when, where, why, and how.	Ms. Palmer gave her history class a lesson on cultural change and the role of ethics. After the lesson she asked the class to work in small groups and then outline ideas.
Expectation Violation: List actions only, no judgments, and lots of verbs—that is, tone of voice, body language, word choice, etc.	At first, Garrison, appeared energized and able to process complex ideas, and frequently contributed to his group. However, Garrison lost interest when it was time to outline his ideas on paper and quickly became withdrawn..
Impact: The consequence of the behavior on the audience.	Ms. Palmer worried that Garrison might be having trouble organizing his ideas and may fall behind in class.

Strategy: *Building on student strengths*
Ms. Palmers created an oral presenter role in each group so that Garrison can still contribute and earn points for asking and answering questions orally.
Outcome:
Garrison is able to positively contribute to his group and Ms. Palmer's class while sharpening his outlining skills by listening and working with his teammates.

3. Use the completed "Black Male Behavioral Intervention Plan" (Table 7.5) as a model to fill out your own blank "Black Male Behavioral Observation Intervention Plan" (Table 7.6, *SBI format adapted from Coaching 101) using the information you have learned from *Mindful Teaching Practices for Black Male Achievement* and your idealized intended strategy and desired outcomes.

REFERENCES

Majors, R., and Billson, J. M. (1992). *Cool pose: The dilemmas of Black manhood in America.* New York: Lexington Books.

Ransaw, T. S. (2013). *The art of being cool: The pursuit of Black masculinity.* Chicago: African American Images.

Watzlawick, P., Beavin Bavelas, J., and Jackson, D. (1967). Some tentative axioms of communication. In *Pragmatics of human communication: A study of interactional patterns, pathologies and paradoxes.* New York: Norton.

Wilkins, A. C. (2008). *Wannabes, goths, and Christians: The boundaries of sex, style, and status.* Chicago: University of Chicago Press.

Black Male Student Efficacy Survey

Theodore S. Ransaw, PhD

Background: One might think that academic identity and race are interrelated. However, students who report a high degree of internalized racial identity also report that racial identity attitudes do not influence their academic

Table 7.6. Blank Behavioral Intervention Plan Practices

Situation: Very specific; who, what, when, where, why, and how.
Behavior: List actions only, no judgments, and lots of verbs—that is, tone of voice, body language, word choice etc.
Impact: The consequence of the behavior on the audience.
Strategy:
Outcome:

progress (Williams & Leonard, 1988). Welch and Hodges (1997) define academic identity as "the personal commitment to a standard of excellence, the willingness to persist in the challenge, struggle, excitement and disappointment intrinsic in the learning process" (p. 37). As defined by DeCandia (2014), academic identity is viewed a a construct of future orientation, self-efficacy, confidence in academic abilities, and grit. Paying attention to self-efficacy may be the missing link that predicts academic achievement for African American students. In Knapp, Kelly-Reid, Whitmore, and Miller's (2007) research, academic self-efficacy was the strongest predictor of first-year college performance for high-achieving African American students who attended predominantly White institutions (PWIs). In their study, self-efficacy was a stronger predictor of academic achievement than traditional measures of high school GPA and combined SAT scores (Knapp et al., 2007).

Objectives: To build upon or increase student engagement in ways that affirm Black male identity.

Outcomes: To support positive Black male student and teacher relationships by providing teachers with background information about how Black males in their classrooms feel about their ability to succeed in school.

Table 7.7. Black Male Student Efficacy Survey

1	I believe that it is cool to be smart.	Y/N
2	I feel good when I get a good grade.	Y/N
3	I feel bad when I get a bad grade.	Y/N
4	I am interested in learning more than getting good grades.	Y/N
5	Sometimes I hide the fact that I don't understand.	Y/N
6	I believe smart people do not have to work hard.	Y/N
7	I think the more time I spend on homework the higher my grades will be.	Y/N
8	I feel that my teacher(s) cares about me.	Y/N
9	I feel that my teacher(s) knows when I do not understand.	Y/N
10	I like to answer questions out loud in class.	Y/N
11	I like it when the teacher asks me to do math on the board.	Y/N
12	I like it when the teacher asks me to read out loud.	
13	It is important to me that I look good in front of my friends.	Y/N
14	I believe that I can ask the teacher(s) questions when I need help.	Y/N
15	I feel that if I try hard enough I can get it.	Y/N
16	When I read, it is easy for me to tell when I do not understand. *Not Sure	Somewhat Sure	Pretty Sure	Very Sure*	
17	When I answer a math problem, it is easy for me to tell when I do not understand. *Not Sure	Somewhat Sure	Pretty Sure	Very Sure*	
18	I am sure that I did well in reading this year. *Not Sure	Somewhat Sure	Pretty Sure	Very Sure*	

19 I am sure that I did well in math this year.
    Not Sure | Somewhat Sure | Pretty Sure | Very Sure
20 I am sure that my teachers(s) give me more good feedback than bad.
    Not Sure | Somewhat Sure | Pretty Sure | Very Sure
21 I am sure that my teacher(s) makes me feel that I can understand the lesson most
    of the time.
    Not Sure | Somewhat Sure | Pretty Sure | Very Sure
22 I understand what it takes to do well in school.
    Do Not Understand | Somewhat Understand | Understand | Clearly Understand
23 I clearly understand how to use math in everyday life.
    Do Not Understand | Somewhat Understand | Understand | Clearly Understand
    I clearly understand the steps it takes to get to college.
    Do Not Understand | Somewhat Understand | Understand | Clearly Understand

DIRECTIONS

1. Ask your Black male students to read the survey (Table 7.7) and circle Y for Yes or N for No.
2. Let your students know they do not need to put their name on the survey.
3. Collect the completed surveys, tally the results, and make curriculum and school adaptations based on the results.

REFERENCES

DeCandia, G. M. (2014). *Relationships between academic identity and academic achievement in low-income urban adolescents.* (Doctoral dissertation). Rutgers University, Graduate School of Applied and Professional Psychology.

Knapp, L. G., Kelly-Reid, J. E., Whitmore, R. W., and Miller, E. (2007). *Enrollment in postsecondary institutions, fall 2005; graduation rates, 1999 and 2002 cohorts; and financial statistics, fiscal year 2005* (Publication No. NCES 2007–154). Washington, DC: National Center for Education Statistics, US Department of Education. Retrieved from http://nces.ed.gov/pubsearch/pubsinfo. asp?pubid_2007154.

Ransaw, T., and Majors, R. (Eds.). (2016). *Closing education achievement gaps for African American males.* East Lansing: Michigan State University Press.

Welch, O. M., and Hodges, C. R. (1997). *Standing outside on the inside.* Albany, NY: State University of New York Press.

Williams, T. M., and Leonard, M. M. (1988, January). Graduating black undergraduates: The step beyond retention. *Journal of College Student Development*, 69–75.

High School Equity Survey

Theodore S. Ransaw, PhD

Background: Because humans are social beings and social beings organize themselves into groups, hierarchies occur frequently. The thinking behind hierarchies is that humans naturally organize themselves into groups based on the instinct to survive. Humans who grouped together in the past lived to have descendants today. The instinct to belong to a group is strong, and the desire for a social status found in groups is so powerful that it is often unconscious. In fact, social status can be measured in the brain even when sleeping. The part of the brain connected to social status is directly related to the group's size that one belongs and how much a person interacts with that group. Additionally, the ability to identify and maintain social hierarchies can be clearly identified in the amygdala, the hypothalamus, the temporal lobe, and the prefrontal cortex (Schjelderup-Ebbe, 1922; Watanabe & Yamamoto, 2015). The impact of a person's positive or negative sense of social status is so strong that having low social or economic status can lead to anxiety and depression (Hoebel et al., 2017).

Brown (2004) maintains that adolescence is a period when less time is spent with parents, more time is spent with friends, and peer relationships become more complex. In other words, the brain is hardwired to respond to social networks while students transition from middle school to high school. In addition, adolescence is also a time when the brain activates reward feelings when peers are around. Consequently, the pressure to conform to the norm is increased during adolescence. Peers who are slightly older and more attractive and have better social skills and higher status are more influential (Akins, Simon, & Prinstein, 2010). Unfortunately, not all influences are positive, and schools reflect society. In both spaces, race is often tied to social status.

For example, most people view Whiteness as a sign of affluence even though poor Blacks and Whites are more similar in economic terms than different. Consequently, any disruption to social status can trigger negative reactions based on racial and social biases. Intercultural achievement gaps persist between both *high* academically achieving White students in affluent neighborhoods and *high* academically achieving White students from low-socioeconomic-status schools (Plucker, Hardesty, & Burroughs, 2014). That means that academic achievement can be measured differently depending on the school's criteria and social economic status, not just for Black and White schools but also for White schools. It is no wonder that the testing gap in standardized test scores of affluent and low-income students is double the gap between Blacks and Whites (Tavernis, 2012).

Objectives: To build upon or increase student engagement in ways that affirm Black male identity.

Outcomes: To support positive Black male student and teacher relationships by providing teachers with background information about how Black males in their classrooms feel about equity in their school.

DIRECTIONS

1. Ask your Black male students to read the survey (Table 7.8) and circle Y for Yes or N for No.
2. Let your students know they do not need to put their name on the survey.
3. Collect the completed surveys, tally the results, and make curriculum and school adaptations based on the results.

REFERENCES

Akins, J. W., Simon, V. A., & Prinstein, M. J. (2010). Romantic partner selection and socialization of young adolescents' substance use and behavior problems. *Journal of Adolescence,* 33, 813–26.

Brown, B. B. (2004). Adolescents' relationships with peers. In R. M. Lerner and L. Steinberg (Eds.), *Handbook of adolescent psychology* (2nd ed., pp. 363–94). Hoboken, NJ: Wiley.

Hoebel, J., Maske, U. E., Zeeb, H., and Lampert, T. (2017). Social inequalities and depressive symptoms in adults: The role of objective and subjective socioeconomic status. *PLoS ONE, 12*(1): e0169764. https://doi.org/10.1371/journal.pone.0169764.

Plucker, J. A., Hardesty, J., and Burroughs, N. (2014). *Talent on the sidelines: Excellence gaps and America's persistent talent underclass.* Storrs, CT: Center for Education Policy Analysis, University of Connecticut. Retrieved from http://cepa.uconn.edu/mindthegap.

Schjelderup-Ebbe, T. (1922). The pecking order of chickens. *Science, 126,* 1242–43.

Tavernis, S. (2012). Education gap grows between rich and poor, studies say. *New York Times.* Retrieved December 27, 2012, from www.nytimes.com/2012/02/10/education/education-gap-grows-between-rich-and-poor-studies-show.html.

Watanabe, N., and Yamamoto, M. (2015). Neural mechanisms of social dominance. *Frontiers in Neuroscience, 9,* 154. https://doi.org/10.3389/fnins.2015.00154.

Middle School Equity Survey

Theodore S. Ransaw, PhD

Background: Brown (2004) maintains that adolescence is a period when less time is spent with parents, more time is spent with friends, and peer relationships become more complex. In other words, the brain is hardwired to respond to social networks at the same time students transition from middle school to high school. In addition, adolescence is also a time when the brain

Table 7.8. High School Equity Survey

	Boy, Girl, Other	B/G/O
1.	I feel that my teacher(s) cares about me.	Y/N
2.	I feel that my school cares about me.	Y/N
3.	I feel that my teacher(s) treat me fairly.	Y/N
4.	I feel that my school treats me fairly.	Y/N
5.	I feel that my teacher(s) understands the way I talk.	Y/N
6.	I feel that my teacher(s) understands my race.	Y/N
7.	I feel that my teacher(s) understands my culture.	Y/N
8.	I feel that my teacher(s) understands my gender.	Y/N
9.	I feel that my teacher(s) understands my religion.	Y/N
10.	I feel that my teacher(s) understands my language.	Y/N
11.	I feel that I am able to do well on the assignments I am given.	Y/N
12.	I feel that my teacher(s) knows when I do not understand.	Y/N
13.	I feel welcome at school.	Y/N
14.	I feel that I am valued in school.	Y/N
15.	I feel that I am valued by the other students.	Y/N
16.	I feel that I get enough help at home.	Y/N
17.	I feel that I get enough help at school.	Y/N
18.	I feel that I know why I am in school.	Y/N
19.	I feel that what I am being taught is relevant.	Y/N
20.	I find it easy to get around in my classrooms.	Y/N
21.	I find it easy to get around at school.	Y/N
22.	I feel safe in my classrooms.	Y/N
23.	I feel safe at school.	Y/N
24.	I know there is an adult at my school that I can talk to. *Do Not Know	Somewhat Know	Know	Clearly Know*	
25.	I am certain that my school treats all students fairly. *Not Certain	Somewhat Certain	Certain	Completely Certain*	
26.	I am certain that my culture is well represented in my lessons. *Not Certain	Somewhat Certain	Certain	Completely Certain*	
27.	I am sure that my teacher(s) gives me more good feedback than bad. *Not Sure	Somewhat Sure	Sure	Completely Sure*	
28.	I participate in school activities. *Do Not Participate	Somewhat Participate	Participate	Clearly Participate*	
29.	I am sure that my teacher(s) make(s) me feel that I can understand the lesson most of the time. *Not Sure	Somewhat Sure	Sure	Completely Sure*	
30.	I clearly understand the steps it takes to be college and career ready. *Do Not Understand	Somewhat Understand	Understand	Clearly Understand*	

activates reward feelings when peers are around. Consequently, the pressure to conform to the norm is increased during adolescence, and peers who are slightly older and more attractive and have better social skills and higher status are more influential (Akins, Simon, & Prinstein, 2010). Unfortunately, not all influences are positive, and schools reflect society. In both spaces, race is often tied to social status. Consequently, students can treat other students differently based on perceptions and assumptions of both race and class.

When observations of the social cues of our peers change our behavior, we call that peer influence (Laursen, 2013; Collins & Laursen, 2009). Peer influence can operate in at least four ways: (1) direct peer pressure, (2) indirect peer modeling, (3) normative regulation, and (4) structured opportunities (Brown, 2004). Peer influence is also called peer pressure (Brown, 2004). Peer influence / peer pressure management is housed in the prefrontal cortex of the brain.

Unfortunately, just as peer pressure can be either good or bad, student equitable practices can be influenced positively or negatively by those around them (Cox, 2018).

Objectives: To build upon or increase student engagement in ways that affirm Black male identity.

Outcomes: To support positive Black male student and teacher relationships by providing teachers with background information about how Black males in their classrooms feel about equity in their school.

DIRECTIONS

1. Ask your Black male students to read the survey (Table 7.9) and circle Y for Yes or N for No.
2. Let your students know they do not need to put their name on the survey.
3. Collect the completed surveys, tally the results, and make curriculum and school adaptations based on the results.

REFERENCES

Akins, J. W., Simon, V. A., and Prinstein, M. J. (2010). Romantic partner selection and socialization of young adolescents' substance use and behavior problems. *Journal of Adolescence, 33,* 813–26.

Brown, B. B. (2004). Adolescents' relationships with peers. In R. M. Lerner and L. Steinberg (Eds.), *Handbook of adolescent psychology* (2nd ed., pp. 363–94). Hoboken, NJ: Wiley.

Collins, W. A., and Laursen, B. (2009). Parent-adolescent relationships and influences. In R. M. Lerner and L. Steinberg (Eds.), *Handbook of adolescent psychology* (2nd ed., pp. 331–62). Hoboken, NJ: Wiley.

Cox, S. (2018, December). *Peer pressure changes how teens tackle inequality.* London: Goldsmiths University of London. Retrieved from https://www.gold.ac.uk/news/peer-pressure-and-tackling-inequality/.

Table 7.9. Middle School Equity Survey

Boy, Girl, Other	*B/G/O*
1.	I feel that my teacher(s) cares about me.	Y/N
2.	I feel that my school cares about me.	Y/N
3.	I feel that my teacher(s) treats me fairly.	Y/N
4.	I feel that my school treats me fairly.	Y/N
5.	I feel that my teacher(s) understand me.	Y/N
6.	I feel that my teacher(s) understands people who look like me.	Y/N
7.	I feel that I am able to do well in school.	Y/N
8.	I feel that my teacher(s) knows when I do not understand.	Y/N
9.	I feel welcome at school.	Y/N
10.	I feel that I am valued in school.	Y/N
11.	I feel that I get enough help at home.	Y/N
12.	I feel that I get enough help at school.	Y/N
13.	I feel that I know why I am in school.	Y/N
14.	I feel that I am learning about real life.	Y/N
15.	I find it easy to get around in my classrooms.	Y/N
16.	I find it easy to get around at school.	Y/N
17.	I feel safe in my classrooms.	Y/N
18.	I feel safe at school.	Y/N
19.	I know there is an adult at my school that I can talk to. *Do Not Know | Somewhat Know | Know | Clearly Know*	
20.	I am certain that my school treats people who look like me fairly. *Not Certain | Somewhat Certain | Certain | Completely Certain*	
21.	I am certain that people who look like me are well represented in my lessons. *Not Certain | Somewhat Certain | Certain | Completely Certain*	
22.	I am sure that my teacher(s) give(s) me more good feedback than bad. *Not Sure | Somewhat Sure | Sure | Completely Sure*	
23.	I participate in school activities. *Do Not Participate | Somewhat Participate | Participate | Clearly Participate*	
24.	I am sure that my teacher(s) makes me feel that I can understand the lesson most of the time. *Not Sure | Somewhat Sure | Sure | Completely Sure*	
25.	I clearly understand the steps it takes to get to college. *Do Not Understand | Somewhat Understand | Understand | Clearly Understand*	

Laursen, B. (2013). *Speaking of psychology: The good and the bad of peer pressure.* American Psychological Association. Retrieved from https://www.apa.org/research /action/speaking-of-psychology/peer-pressure.

Including Cultural Norms in Mathematics

Theodore S. Ransaw, PhD

Background: Although we have been taught that numbers are free from bias and have no cultural influences, that is simply not the case. Strictly speaking, if the thoughts of a culture are reflected in language, then the cultural influences of language will influence the way people conceptualize and operationalize math. Numbers, like letters, are symbolic representatives of cultural references that form patterns based on cultural norms. However, not all Indigenous cultures' use of mathematics is valued because it was not viewed as math or science. From village design to clothing, African shapes and designs have consistently used fractal geometry, geometric algorithms, complex numeric systems, and recursions throughout history. For those who doubt that patterns found in African tools, housing construction, and clothing and are just decorative art patterns without purposeful meaning, Englash asserts that unconscious structures and designs are not typically made conscious. Africans "have names for the patterns they observe in shapes and numbers" (Englash, 2005, p. 5). In other words, the creation and articulation of a word to describe an object is a conscious practice, meaning that it is a deliberate action (Trevarthen & Delafield-Butt, 2017). Unfortunately, when numbers and numeracy are taught from a deficit perspective, cultural influences of mathematics can be devalued the same way different languages and ideas are devalued (Nicholson, 1968). The desire for stability, structure, and sameness comforts the oppressor by imposing their worldview and simultaneously convincing the oppressed that they are inferior (Freire, 1970). A perfect example of how cultural knowledge of mathematics is overlooked can be found in Egyptian hieroglyphics.

Objectives: To build upon or increase student comprehension in ways that affirm Black male identity.

Outcomes: To support positive Black male student and teacher relationships by providing a model of how to utilize cultural knowledge to connect with and engage Black males with mathematics.

DIRECTIONS

1. Have your students look over the image of the Eye of Horus (Figure 7.1).
2. Ask your students if they can guess the meaning and intent of the collective and individual shapes that make up the image.
3. Give your students the equations for each of the shapes and ask them to find the sum.

REFERENCES

Eglash, R. (2005). *African fractals: Modern computing and indigenous design.* New Brunswick, NJ: Rutgers University Press.

Freire, P. (1970). *Pedagogy of the oppressed.* New York: Continuum.

Nicholson, C. K. (1968). *Anthropology and Education.* Columbus, OH: Charles E. Merrill.

Trevarthen, C., and Delafield-Butt, J. T. (2017). Development of consciousness. In B. Hopkins, E. Geangu, and S. Linkenauger (Eds.), *Cambridge encyclopedia of child development* (2nd ed., pp. 821–35). Cambridge: Cambridge University Press. Retrieved June 24, 2020, from https://www.researchgate.net/publication/320759520_Development_of_Consciousness.

Exercise:

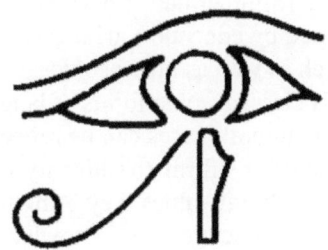

Eye of Horus

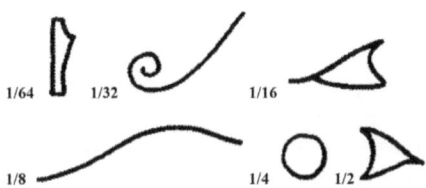

What is the sum of ½ + ¼ + 1/8 + 1/16 + 1/32 + 1/64 =?

Figure 7.1. Eye of Horus

Including Cultural Norms in Reading

Theodore S. Ransaw, PhD

Background: Language is a socially constructed method to express ideas. Unfortunately, sometimes language expresses ideas that are not always spoken out loud. For example, implicit biases, "the automatic yet measurable associations that people have about others, and the behaviors that these associations unconsciously influence" (Mendoza-Denton & Perez, 2020), can cause us to categorize someone as an in-group or outsider-group member (Dovidio & Fiske, 2012). These unconscious biases that separate us from one another are often framed around the languages we speak. One way language is used to categorize people is the separation and preference of high (upper class) and low ways (lower class) of using language and dialect that is influenced by privilege and codified by power, making language a reflection of both race and social class (Smitherman, 1998). So in sum, not only who gets to read and write is classed by education, who gets to say what is correct and what is not correct speech as well as how people speak is correlated to status. And because language is classed, some forms of language are often preferred over others. Class-based cultural biases can be reflected in the classroom.
Objectives: To build upon or affirm the identity of students of color and respect the language and cultural values they bring to the classroom.
Outcomes: The support of student cultural knowledge by providing a model of how to create and implement culturally inclusive perspectives in reading assignments.

DIRECTIONS

1. Find a partner.
2. Read the first paragraph (Figure 7.2) for one minute while your partner highlights words the other mispronounced or skipped. Switch who reads and who highlights and read the first paragraph again.
3. Repeat steps 1 and 2 with the second paragraph (Figure 7.3).
4. Discuss how it might be difficult to read and comprehend reading assignments based on reasons that are not due to your level of intelligence.

Scoring out of 146 words:

1. Take total correct and subtract total incorrect (for example, 3 incorrect − 146 = 143).
2. 143 is your fluency score for today.

3. Were you able to read and understand each paragraph? Share your experience with your partner.

Scoring based on 175 words:

1. Take total correct and subtract total incorrect (for example, 3 incorrect − 175 = 172).
2. 172 is your fluency score for today.
3. Were you able to read and understand each paragraph? Share your experience with your partner.

Paragraph I	
"Molecular approaches to understanding the functional	6
circuitry of the nervous system promise new insights into the	16
relationship between genes, brain and behaviour. The	23
cellular diversity of the brain necessitates a cellular	31
resolution approach towards understanding the functional	37
genomics of the nervous system. We describe here an	46
anatomically comprehensive digital atlas containing the	52
expression patterns of ~20,000 genes in the adult mouse	61
brain. Data were generated using automated high-throughput	69
procedures for *in situ* hybridization and data acquisition, and	78
are publicly accessible online. Newly developed image-	85
based informatics tools allow global genome-scale structural	93
analysis and cross-correlation, as well as identification of	102
regionally enriched genes. Unbiased fine-resolution analysis	109
has identified highly specific cellular markers as well as	118
extensive evidence of cellular heterogeneity not evident in	126
classical neuroanatomical atlases. This highly standardized	132
atlas provides an open, primary data resource for a wide	142
variety of further studies concerning brain organization and	150
function."	151

Borrowed from http://www.nature.com/nature/journal/v445/n7124/full/nature05453.html

Figure 7.2. Paragraph I
Borrowed from http://www.nature.com/nature/journal/v445/n7124/full/nature05453.html.

"When the Aztecs realized that Cortez and his army that was	11
backed by the Tlaxcalans were marching on Tenochitlan,	19
they sent emissaries to the neighboring tribe of the Tarascans	29
for aid. The Tarascans sacrificed the Aztec messengers,	37
and Tenochitlan fell. After he defeated the Aztecs in 1520,	47
Cortez betrayed the Tlaxcalans and then killed the Tarascans	56
as well. The Tarascans had no written form of written	66
communication. So complete was Cortez's elimination	72
of the Tarascans, the only way they are known in history is	84
by the writing of the Aztecs. Consequently, for South	93
Americans, cultural division and cultural division between	100
indigenous people signals not only a cultural death but a	120
physical one as well. Although it is difficult to determine	130
what would have happened to the Nahatul if the Tarascans	140
had helped the Aztecs, or if the Tlaxcalans had never sided	151
with Cortez, the images of the Aztec warrior function as a	162
reminder of the necessity for unity and reciprocal	170
communication in South America. Put simply,	186
Mesoamerican identity in Latin hip-hop promotes vigilance	
against assimilation."	187

Figure 7.3. Paragraph II: Aztecs

Borrowed from Ransaw, T. (2012). Ver y ser visto: To see and be seen in Latin hip-hop. *Words. Beats. Life: The Global Journal of Hip-Hop Culture, 5*(1), 104–118.

REFERENCES

Dovidio, J. F., and Fiske, S. T. (2012). Under the radar: how unexamined biases in decision-making processes in clinical interactions can contribute to health care disparities. *American Journal of Public Health, 102*(5), 945–52. https://doi.org/10.2105/AJPH.2011.300601.

Mendoza-Denton, R., and Perez, A. D. (2020). *Racism and the narrative of biological inevitability*. Othering & Belonging. Retrieved from https://www.otheringandbelonging.org/racism-and-the-narrative-of-biological-inevitability/.

Ransaw, T. (2012). Ver y ser visto: To see and be seen in Latin hip-hop. *Words. Beats. Life: The Global Journal of Hip-Hop Culture, 5*(1), 104–18.

Smitherman, G. (1998). *Talkin that talk.* New York: Routledge.

Black Male Literacy Concept Map

Theodore S. Ransaw, PhD

Background: Literacy Circles Concept Maps are designed for small groups to organize concepts and relationships between themes using students' prior knowledge and experiences. "Literacy education has to have a strong gravitational pull for African American male adolescents [that speaks] in their present-day contexts" (Tatum, 2008, p. 163) to effectively break these gendered and cultural norms. For example, it is possible to engage Black boys in reading by utilizing multifaceted texts that capitalize on both gendered and culturally affirming text in an atmosphere of working in groups (Bean & Ransaw, 2013). Black males seem to thrive in classes to work collectively and are stimulated with variety in their materials and learning environments (Ransaw, 2013; Bonner, 2000).

Objectives: To build upon or increase student literacy, practice writing skills, and facilitate student engagement—making reading/learning fun!

Outcomes: Teacher-student interactions are culturally affirming and demonstrate culturally sensitive instruction that help students make real-world connections by making sense of text through their eyes with their own words.

DIRECTIONS

Have students write each concept on an index card to be placed at the top of a poster board. Write themes related to the concepts on a post-it note so they can be moved around. Draw connections between the themes and concepts, reflect, then draw a final map. Readers share with their classmates what they have learned at the end of the book and what it means in their lives with their own words—that is, rap, poem, dance, song, poster, et cetera. (See example in Figure 7.4.)

REFERENCES

Bean, T., and Ransaw, T. (2013). The masculinity and portrayals of African American boys in young adult literature: A critical deconstruction and reconstruction of this genre. In B. Guzzetti and T. Bean (Eds.), *Adolescent literacies and the gendered self: (Re)constructing identities through multimodal literacy practices*. New York: Routledge.

Bonner, F. A. (2000). African American giftedness: Our nation's deferred dream. *Journal of Black Studies, 30*, 643–63. Retrieved from http://ecs.force.com/studies/rsviewstemL?faq=a080g000019815h.

EXAMPLE

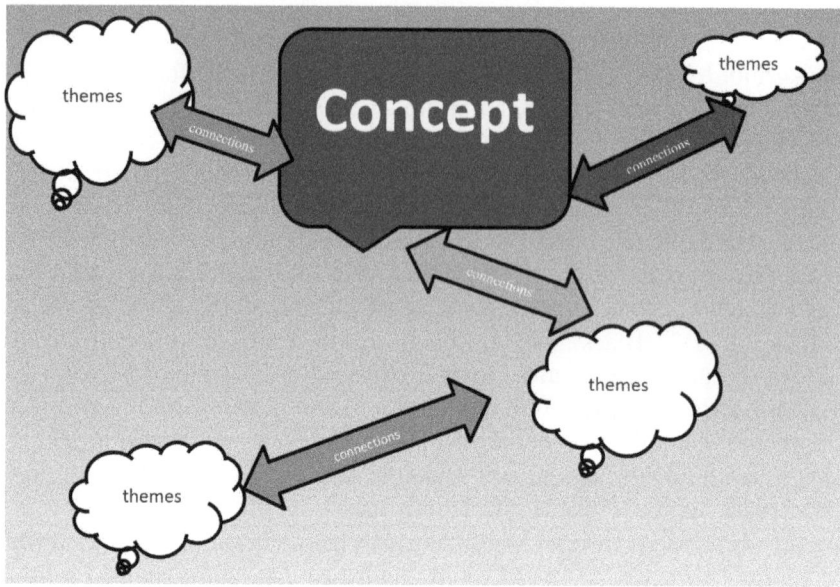

Figure 7.4. Concept Map

Ransaw, T. (2013). *The art of being cool: The pursuit of Black masculinity*. Chicago: African American Images.

Tatum, A. W. (2008). Toward a more anatomically complete model of literacy instruction: A focus on African American male adolescents and texts. *Harvard Educational Review, 78*, 155–80.

RTI/MTSS Effective Teacher Survey

Theodore S. Ransaw, PhD, and Sean Williams, PhD

Background: Most educators are familiar with response to intervention (RTI) (some states utilize multitiered system of supports [MTSS], similar to RTI but it includes behavior interventions). However, a brief background about RTI is a good refresher and also serves as helpful information for parents and community leaders.

RTI is essentially an early detection model for identifying students who are lagging in skill development in comparison to expected development benchmarks (Brown, 2008; Gersten & Dimino, 2006). Emphasis thus far has been on literacy interventions; however, mathematics is slowly becoming the focus of RTI programming as well. To identify deficiencies, schools categorize student achievement data into three levels using a series of tests (known as universal screeners) that evaluate basic skills such as fluency and comprehension. Using this data, students are then divided into three groups based on ability levels. This process of testing and grouping students requires a huge amount of cooperation among school personnel such as administrators, specialists, and teachers. Because many of these tests are given in a one-on-one method, volunteers are usually trained to assist with the testing, and students have to be slotted in for testing appointments. This process requires much planning and staff development. Schools typically devote professional development time to developing an RTI process within the organization.

The first level of RTI's tiered intervention is identified as tier I. In tier I, students need some or no academic interventions to maintain grade-level work. This work is often done in core classrooms, and it requires teachers to deliver core curriculum with specific research-based strategies. In many cases, teachers are not asked to teach more content; instead they are asked to teach their standard content with targeted instructional strategies or methods of delivery.

Tier II identifies students who need more specific and intense instruction. This instruction is often delivered to students in small groups, in addition to the instruction they receive in general core classes. Tier II students are sorted through testing data, such as fluency and universal comprehension screeners (tests).

Tier III, the final level, consists of students who need the most support. These students typically have a learning disability and require small group or one-on-one instruction, and they receive support using a research-based program designed for their specific deficiencies. For students to move down from one tier to another tier, they must demonstrate proficiency on a variety of targeted assessments (Fuchs & Fuchs, 2006). Student achievement is also continually monitored throughout the year to assure the intervention strategies are appropriate and effective by frequently monitoring the progress of each individual student. By using RTI instructional strategies, classroom teachers become more accustomed to viewing instruction as an individualistic process rather than as a group process. Teachers are more aware of students' academic deficiencies and can adjust their lesson planning throughout the year to help improve academic achievement (Williams, 2016, p. 83).

With the understanding that schools have limited time and resources, it is highly likely that schools would adopt a uniform system like RTI or MTSS to meet the requirements of these multiple accountability programs. As schools implement RTI, there is a danger that African American males are overidentified into RTI programs at an excessive rate to their White counterparts. Due to this potential imbalance and the important tool that RTI represents, the relationship between RTI programs in schools and African American males should be studied. (Williams, 2016, p. 90).

Objectives: To build upon or increase student engagement in ways that affirm Black male identity.

Outcomes: To support positive Black male student and teacher relationships by providing principals and superintendents with background information about how teachers in their classrooms feel about their RTI/MTSS training and support.

DIRECTIONS

1. Read *Mindful Teaching Practices for Black Male Achievement.*
2. Ask teachers to read the survey (Table 7.10) and circle their choices. *Let teachers know they do not need to put their name on the survey.*
3. Collect the completed surveys, tally the results, and make suggestions to sustain and enhance data-based strategies to increase RTI/MTSS training to support Black male academic success based on the results.

REFERENCE

Brown, J., & Doolittle, J. (2008). A cultural, linguistic, and ecological framework for response to intervention with English language learners. *Teaching Exceptional Children, 40*(5), 66–72.

Table 7.10. RTI/MTSS Effective Teacher Survey

1	Did the teacher implement differentiated instruction based on student achievement data?				
	1	2	3	4	5
	Strongly agree	Agree	Neutral	Disagree	Strongly disagree
2	Does the teacher regularly update and reassess benchmark levels?				
	1	2	3	4	5
	Strongly agree	Agree	Neutral	Disagree	Strongly disagree
3	Has the teacher been given the resources and training needed to implement changes?				
	1	2	3	4	5
	Strongly agree	Agree	Neutral	Disagree	Strongly disagree
4	Do teachers provide opportunities for students with similar issues to work in groups?				
	1	2	3	4	5
	Strongly agree	Agree	Neutral	Disagree	Strongly disagree

5   Is the principal the instructional leader of the school?

1	2	3	4	5
Strongly agree	Agree	Neutral	Disagree	Strongly disagree

6   Does the teacher try to adapt to the students' learning style?

1	2	3	4	5
Strongly agree	Agree	Neutral	Disagree	Strongly disagree

7   Do the school climate and district policies promote data-driven differentiated learning practices?

1	2	3	4	5
Strongly agree	Agree	Neutral	Disagree	Strongly disagree

8   Does school/district leadership meet regularly to evaluate data-driven differentiated instruction?

1	2	3	4	5
Strongly agree	Agree	Neutral	Disagree	Strongly disagree

9   Does the school/district offer continuous professional development for its teachers?

1	2	3	4	5
Strongly agree	Agree	Neutral	Disagree	Strongly disagree

Fuchs, D., & Fuchs, L. S. (2006). Introduction to Response to Intervention: What, why, and how valid is it? *Reading Research Quarterly, 41*(1), 93–99. https://doi.org/10.1598/RRQ.41.1.4.

Gersten, R., & Dimino, J. A. (2006). RTI (Response to Intervention): Rethinking special education for students with reading difficulties (yet again). *Reading Research Quarterly, 41*(1), 99–108. https://doi.org/10.1598/RRQ.41.1.5.

Williams, S. (2016). Using response to intervention effectively with African American males. In T. Ransaw and R. Major (Eds.), *Closing education achievement gaps for African American males.* East Lansing, MI: Michigan State University Press.

RTI/MTSS Implementation Survey

Sean Williams, PhD, and Theodore Ransaw, PhD

Background: Most educators are familiar with response to intervention (RTI) (some states utilize multitiered system of supports [MTSS], similar to RTI but it includes behavior interventions). However, a brief background about RTI is a good refresher and also serves as helpful information for parents and community leaders.

RTI is essentially an early detection model for identifying students who are lagging in skill development in comparison to expected development benchmarks (Brown, 2008; Gersten & Dimino, 2006). Emphasis thus far has been on literacy interventions; however, mathematics is slowly becoming the focus of RTI programming as well. To identify deficiencies, schools categorize student achievement data into three levels using a series of tests (known as universal screeners) that evaluate basic skills such as fluency and comprehension. Using this data, students are then divided into three groups based on ability levels. This process of testing and grouping students requires a huge amount of cooperation among school personnel such as administrators, specialists, and teachers. Because many of these tests are given in a one-on-one method, volunteers are usually trained to assist with the testing, and students have to be slotted in for testing appointments. This process requires much planning and staff development. Schools typically devote professional development time to developing an RTI process within the organization.

The first level of RTI's tiered intervention is identified as tier I. In tier I, students need some or no academic interventions to maintain grade-level work. This work is often done in core classrooms, and it requires teachers to deliver core curriculum with specific research-based strategies. In many cases, teachers are not asked to teach more content; instead they are asked to teach their standard content with targeted instructional strategies or methods of delivery.

Tier II identifies students who need more specific and intense instruction. This instruction is often delivered to students in small groups, in addition to the instruction they receive in general core classes. Tier II students are sorted through testing data, such as fluency and universal comprehension screeners (tests).

Tier III, the final level, consists of students who need the most support. These students typically have a learning disability and require small group or one-on-one instruction, and they receive support using a research-based program designed for their specific deficiencies. For students to move down from one tier to another tier, they must demonstrate proficiency on a variety of targeted assessments (Fuchs & Fuchs, 2006). Student achievement is also continually monitored throughout the year to assure the intervention strategies are appropriate and effective by frequently monitoring the progress of each individual student. By using RTI instructional strategies, classroom teachers become more accustomed to viewing instruction as an individualistic process rather than as a group process. Teachers are more aware of students' academic deficiencies and can adjust their lesson planning throughout the year to help improve academic achievement (Williams, 2016, p. 83).

With the understanding that schools have limited time and resources, it is highly likely that schools would adopt a uniform system like RTI or MTSS to meet the requirements of these multiple accountability programs. As schools implement RTI, there is a danger that African American males are overidentified into RTI programs at an excessive rate to their White counterparts. Due to this potential imbalance and the important tool that RTI represents, the

Table 7.11. RTI/MTSS Implementation Survey

1	I understand the difference between RTI/MTSS and special education.	Y/N
2	I believe that RTI/MTSS can be used to help uncover behavioral problems for students who are not being challenged enough.	Y/N
3	I am aware that RTI/MTSS are also helpful for students who are high achieving.	Y/N
4	I understand that RTI/MTSS placements are based on specified student achievement data.	Y/N
5	I feel that I have had enough training to teach RTI/MTSS-driven lessons.	Y/N
6	I feel that my principal and I are on the same page regarding RTI/MTSS.	Y/N
7	I feel that I have the resources and materials needed to successfully implement RTI/MTSS.	Y/N
8	I feel that I have the support needed to successfully implement RTI/MTSS.	Y/N
9	I feel that parents are aware of our current RTI/MTSS program.	Y/N
10	I believe that RTI/MTSS can play a crucial role in closing achievement gaps.	Y/N
11	I feel that my colleagues understand and support RTI/MTSS as a method for closing the achievement gap.	Y/N
12	I feel that I am aware of the average length of time for student tier movements of the students in my class.	Y/N

relationship between RTI programs in schools and African American males should be studied (Williams, 2016, p. 90).

Objectives: To build upon or increase student engagement in ways that affirm Black male identity.

Outcomes: To support positive Black male student and teacher relationships by providing principals, superintendents, and school board members with background information about how teachers feel about their background, training, and support surrounding RTI/MTSS.

DIRECTIONS

1. Let teachers know they do not need to put their name on the survey.
2. Ask teachers to read the survey (Table 7.11) and circle their choice.
3. Collect the completed surveys, tally the results, and make suggestions to sustain and enhance data-based strategies to increase Black male academic success based on the results.

REFERENCE

Brown, J., & Doolittle, J. (2008). A cultural, linguistic, and ecological framework for response to intervention with English language learners. *Teaching Exceptional Children, 40*(5), 66–72.

Fuchs, D., & Fuchs, L. S. (2006). Introduction to Response to Intervention: What, why, and how valid is it? *Reading Research Quarterly, 41*(1), 93–99. https://doi.org/10.1598/RRQ.41.1.4.

Gersten, R., & Dimino, J. A. (2006). RTI (Response to Intervention): Rethinking special education for students with reading difficulties (yet again). *Reading Research Quarterly, 41*(1), 99–108. https://doi.org/10.1598/RRQ.41.1.5.

Williams, S. (2016). Using response to intervention effectively with African American males. In T. Ransaw and R. Major (Eds.), *Closing education achievement gaps for African American males.* East Lansing, MI: Michigan State University Press.

Appendix

HELPFUL WEBSITES

12 Things White People Can Do Now Because of Ferguson
An Alternet article about social justice activism
http://www.alternet.org/news-amp-politics/12-things-white-people-can-do
-now-because-ferguson

African-American Experience and Issues of Race and Racism in U.S. Schools
Provides a link to other websites that cover African American experience and issues of race and racism, in U.S. schools
http://www.ithaca.edu/wise/race_african_american/

Are There Really More Black Men In Prison Than College?
A National Public Radio segment on the truth about Black males
http://www.npr.org/2013/04/23/178601467/are-there-really-more-Black-men
-in-prison-than-college

Black boys of distinction
A Facebook group that sports Black males
https://www.facebook.com/InspiringBlackBoysTowardManhood

Black Men & Depression: The Top 8 Signs
A Black doctor blog about Black male healthcare
http://Blackdoctor.org/2327/Black-men-depression-the-top-8-signs/

Black Male Depression
A blog page about health issues in the Black community

http://www.indianapolisrecorder.com/health/article_3499c65a-ecb7-11e3
-9bb1-0019bb2963f4.html

Black students more likely to be suspended –even in preschool
A CBS News video link about Black students and schooling
http://www.cbsnews.com/news/education-department-Black-preschoolers
-more-likely-to-be-suspended/.

Concerned Black men
A national organization that connects underserved youth with resources and role models
http://www.cbmnational.org/

Dismantling the School-To-Prison-Pipeline Game
An online game that illustrates the futility of zero-tolerance policies
https://www.aclu.org/school-prison-pipeline-game

Epidemic Depression in Young Black Men
A blog page by African American therapists
http://africanamericantherapists.com/about-therapy/do-you-need-therapy/
depression/Black-men-and-depression/epidemic-depression-in-young-Black
-men/#sthash.xyDbgwZY.dpbs

The Good Father: African American Fathers Who Positively Influence the Educational Outcomes of Their Children
Academic journal article highlighting positive aspects of Black male fathers
http://www.jstor.org/stable/10.2979/spectrum.2.2.1

Help Your Child Manage Traumatic Events
A blog page from the Anxiety and Depression Association of America
http://www.adaa.org/living-with-anxiety/children-and-teens/tips-parents-and
-caregivers/help-your-child-manage-traumatic-

How to Prevent Depression in Children
A wiki page with full references
http://www.wikihow.com/Prevent-Depression-in-Children

Leading by example: Black male teachers make students "feel proud."
A Hechinger Report article about inspiring Black males
http://hechingerreport.org/leading-by-example-black-male-teachers-make
-students-feel-proud/

Mothers of Black boys
A Black mother's organization that is working to eradicate negative stereotypes of Black boys
http://mothersofBlackboys.org/

The Myth of the Absent Black Father
A Think Progress article detailing the truth about Black fathers
http://thinkprogress.org/health/2014/01/16/3175831/myth-absent-Black-father/

NAACP Criminal Justice Fact Sheet
A resource guide about criminal justice inequities by one of America's oldest organizations
http://www.naacp.org/pages/criminal-justice-fact-sheet

New Research Takes Aim at Stereotype That Black Young Men Are Not College Material
A National Journal article that discusses eliminating negative stereotypes about Young Black men
http://news.yahoo.com/research-takes-aim-stereotype-black-young-men-not-133028381--politics.html

Prostate Cancer Survivor Ken Griffey Sr. & Ken Griffey Jr. Help Men Make Uncomfortable Conversations "Normal"
A father and son blog about Black male health
http://blackdoctor.org/480893/prostate-cancer-survivor-ken-griffey-sr-ken-griffey-jr-are-helping-men-make-uncomfortable-conversations-normal/

Science Genius
A STEM program that uses hip-hop for motivating young Black students
http://genius.com/artists/Science-genius

Tips for Parents and Caregivers
Advice about childcare from the Anxiety and Depression Association of America
http://www.adaa.org/living-with-anxiety/children/tips-parents-and-caregivers

ALLIES

American Center for Law & Justice (ACLJ
American Civil Liberties Union ACLU

Better Government Association
Black Lives Matter
Center for Individual Freedom (CFIF)
Coalition for Juvenile Justice
Common Cause
Constitution Project
Democracy Matters
Ella Baker Center for Human Rights
Food & Water Watch
Foundation for Individual Rights in Education
Illinois Innocence Project
Institute for Justice
Judicial Watch
National Alliance of Latin American and Caribbean Communities
National Center for Reason and Justice
Project Vote Smart
Southern Poverty Law Center SPLC
U.S. Department of Education
Youth Justice Work Groups

BLACK MALE FRATERNITIES

Alpha Phi Alpha
Beta Phi Pi Gamma Psi Gamma
Delta Psi Chi Swordsmen
Gamma Psi Beta
Iota Phi Theta
Kappa Alpha Psi
Lambda Chi Epsilon
Malik Sigma Psi
Megiste Arete
Omega Psi Phi
Phi Beta Sigma
Phi Delta Phi Rho
Phi Rho Eta
Sigma Phi Rho
Sigma Pi Phi

HISTORICALLY BLACK COLLEGES AND UNIVERSITIES

Alcorn
Bethune-Cookman University
Bowie State University
Claflin University
Delaware State University
Dillard University
Elizabeth City State University
Fayetteville State University
Fisk University
Florida Agricultural and Mechanical University
Hampton University
Howard University
Jackson State University
Johnson C. Smith University
Lincoln University of Pennsylvania
Morehouse College
Norfolk State University
North Carolina A&T State University
North Carolina Central University
Oakwood University
Philander Smith College
Prairie View A&M University
Spelman College
Tougaloo College
Tuskegee University
University of Maryland Eastern Shore
Virginia State University
Virginia University of Lynchburg
Wilberforce University
Winston-Salem State University
Xavier University of Louisiana

RECOMMENDED BOOKS FOR TEACHERS AND MENTORS

200+ Educational Strategies to Teach Children of Color. Chicago: African American Images; 1 edition, by Jawana Kunjufu

Afrocentricity: The Theory of Social Change, by Molefi Kete Asante

The Ankh: African Origins of Electromagnetism, by Amen Ankh Nub

The Art of Being Cool: The Pursuit of Black Masculinity, by Theodore Ransaw

At the Cross Roads of Fear and Freedom: The Fight for Educational and Social Justice, by Robert L. Green

Black Athena: The Afroasiatic Roots of Classical Civilization (The Fabrication of Ancient Greece 1785–1985, Volume 1), by Martin Benal

Educating Black Males: Critical Lessons in Schooling, Community, and Power, by Ronnie Hopkins

Expect the Most Provide the Best, by Robert L. Green

From the Browder File Vol II: Survival Strategies for Africans in America: 13 Steps to Freedom, by Antony Browder

Math Dictionary for Kids, by T. Fitzgerald

The Mis-Education of the Negro, by B. T. Washington

The Negro Problem, by Booker T. Washington

The New Black Man, by Mark Anthony Neal

Nile Valley Contributions to Civilization: Exploding the Myths, by Antony Browder

The Philadelphia Negro: A Social Study, by W. E. B. DuBois

Smartphones: A Mobile Platform for Greater Learning, Equity and Success, by Kevin Green

Stolen Legacy: Greek Philosophy is Stolen Egyptian Philosophy, by George James

The Teachings of Ptahhotep: The Oldest Book in the World, by Asa G. Hilliard III

Through Ebony Eyes: What Teachers Need to Know But Are Afraid to Ask About African-American Students, by Gail Thompson

WRITING LETTERS FOR IMPLEMENTING POSTIVE CHANGE FOR BLACK MALES

We have all heard the phrase that the pen is mightier than the sword. It's true! One of the most powerful tools to make a difference in the lives of Black males is to write a letter. Although we live in a digital age where people write mails, blogs, and text, the written word still makes a difference. Here below we have crafted a few suggestions and tips for writing to stakeholders and politicians.

Parent to Teacher Letter-Writing Tips

- While there are some overarching guidelines, such as making sure you use the correct heading, title, address, and return address, the best letters are the ones written in your own words.
- Make sure you mention the name of the child that you are a parent of.
- Try to use objective language that does not make the teacher seem uncaring or uncommitted.
- Clearly state the topic, thank you letter, absence letter for schools who need an official document for absences, rrequests for more challenging homework, et cetera.
- Provide something personal about your son that is helpful to a teacher.
- Mention the possible potential outcomes that may happen if something is changed.
- Include a call to action, how you envision the change to look like.

Sample Parent Letter to Teacher

Your Name
321 Street
Your City AA 12468

School Name
123 Street
Anywhere city, BB, 84621

Date

Dear Ms. Edwards,

Hopefully, you will remember me. I'm Marcus's father Bryan Boggs. I just wanted to let you know how much Marcus enjoys being in your class. He comes home excited about what he has learned and well prepared to do his homework.

As I mentioned at our parent-teacher conference at the beginning of the year, the school has been hard for Marcus. He is a very active and bright kid. He was constantly finishing his assignments before the others in his last class and would get up and walk around looking for something else to do. So, we homeschooled him for a while. That didn't seem to work at all. Marcus continued to excel with homeschooling, even skipping a grade, but he missed having friends. You are the first teacher he has had that keeps him mentally occupied and challenged.

You are truly a standout teacher. You have made learning relevant and fun. Thank you for a great school year. Also, don't forget, I am off on Tuesdays and Wednesdays in case you need a volunteer.

Sincerely,

(Place your name here)

***

Parent to Police Tips for Writing a Letter to the Police Chief

While there are some overarching guidelines, such as making sure you use the correct heading, title, address, and return address, the best letters are the ones written in your own words.

Describe your concern, why you are interested and what the impacts of the issue are.

Provide an example of your concern in relation to your issue or issues.

Suggest a call to action or possible solution.

Finish with a sentence that warmly invites the police chief to respond.

***

Letter to Police Chief Template

Your Name
321 Street
Your City AA 12468

Representative Name
123 Street
Anywhere city, BB, 84621

Date

Dear Police Chief [or Sherriff, full name],

School policies such as zero-tolerance policies are of interest to me because I am a White mother of a Black son, Christopher Warren. Chris's school [name of school] has a "tough-on-crime" policy, which has resulted in increased surveillance of Black boys. Chris has been a victim of biased observations coming and going to school. I have seen police officers stop and question him. Not because he was doing something wrong, but because we live in a predominately White neighborhood. With the recent increase of attacks on Black boys across the United States, I have taken to walking Chris to school and back, even though we live only two blocks from the school.

I am primarily concerned that is being stereotyped and that the resulting biases will dissuade him from having a positive attitude toward law enforcement in the future. Since he is wary of police officers at such a young age now, it may cause him to seek help when he really needs it. In an effort to encourage goodwill between police officers and students, I suggest that someone from the department have a school, assembly, or classroom visit at the school in the near future.

I realize that making Chris feel unsafe at school may not have been the intent of the police officers who stopped my son. I also get the impression that you are an advocate for child safety. Therefore I look forward to reading your response or attending a school presentation with you or one of your officers.

Sincerely,

(Place your name here)
Concerned parent

***

Citizen to Politician Tips for Writing a Letter to a State Representative

While there are some overarching guidelines, such as making sure you use the correct heading, title, address, and return address, the best letters are the ones written in your own words.

Make sure you mention that you are in their district.

Try not to blame the legislator or an individual. Use language that is objective and specific without being accusatory.

Clearly state the topic, zero-tolerance policies, housing issues, health policy concerns, et cetera. . .

Provide something personal as to why your subject matters.

Mention the possible implications of what could happen to your district if nothing is changed.

Include a call to action, what you would like done, that is, change in legislation.

***

State Representative Sample Letter

Your Name
321 Street
Your City AA 12468

Representative Name
123 Street
Anywhere city, BB, 84621

(Place date here)

The Honorable Senator Brian Chapin,

My name is William Leeland, a resident of your district. I write to inform you that zero-tolerance policies are destroying the Black community. Here in our district, Blacks students makeup about 10 percent of the population but makeup 50 percent of the students suspended and expelled.

Last week my nephew came to school with a Pop-Tart in his backpack. Just before lunch, he took out the Pop-Tart and shaped it into a gun. He was suspended for assault.

As I mentioned at our parent-teacher conference at the beginning of the year, the school has been hard for Marcus. He is a very active and bright kid. He was constantly finishing his assignments before the others in his last class and would get up and walk around looking for something else to do. So we homeschooled him for a while. That didn't seem to work at all. Marcus continued to excel with homeschooling, even skipping a grade, but he missed having friends. You are the first teacher he has had that keeps him mentally occupied and challenged.

You are truly a standout teacher. You have made learning relevant and fun. Thank you for a great school year. Also, don't forget, I am off on Tuesdays and Wednesdays in case you need a volunteer.

Sincerely,

(Place your name here)

References

ACLU. (2001, February). *ACLU files a lawsuit on behalf of Maine high school students expelled for taking a pain reliever.* Retrieved from https://www.aclu.org/press-releases/aclu-files-lawsuit-behalf-maine-high-school-student-expelled-taking-pain-reliever.

Albright, G. W. (1937/2016). *George Washington Albright: Mississippi slave narratives from the WPA Records.* MSGenWeb Slave Narrative Project. Retrieved from http://msgw.org/slaves/albright.pdf.

Alegría, M., Lin, J. Y., Green, J. G., Sampson, N. A., Gruber, M. J., and Kessler, R. C. (2012). Role of referrals in mental health service disparities for racial and ethnic minority youth. *Journal of the American Academy of Child Adolescent Psychiatry, 51*(7), 703–11.e2. https://doi.org/10.1016/j.jaac/2012.05.005.

Alexander, D. R. (2009). *What's so special about special education? A critical study of White general education teachers' perceptions regarding the referrals of African American students for special education services.* Texas A&M University. ProQuest Dissertations and Theses, 159. Retrieved from http://ezproxy.msu.edu/login?url=http://search.proquest.com/docview/305124369?accountid=12598. (305124369).

Allen, W. (1987). Black colleges vs. White colleges: The fork in the road for Black students. *Change, 19*(3), 28–34.

Allen, W. R. (1992). The color of success: African American college student outcomes at predominantly White and historically Black public colleges and universities. *Harvard Educational Review, 62*(1), 26–44.

Allen, W. R., Epps, E. G., and Haniff, N. Z. (Eds). (1991). *College in Black and White: African American students in predominantly White and historically Black public universities.* Albany: State University of New York Press.

Almasy, S., and Yan, H. (2014, November). *Protesters fill streets across the country as Ferguson's protest spread coast to coast.* CNN. Retrieved from http://www.cnn.com/2014/11/25/us/national-ferguson-protests/index.html.

American Civil Liberties Union. (2017). *Bullies in blue: The origins and consequences of school policing.* ACLU Foundation. Retrieved from https://www.aclu.org/sites/default/files/field_document/aclu_bullies_in_blue_4_11_17_final.pdf.

Anderson, V. (2021, May). *Education usually improves health: But racism sabotages benefits for Black men.* NPR. Retrieved from https://www.npr.org/sections /health-shots/2021/05/18/996577905/racism-derails-black-mens-health-even-as -education-levels-rise.

Arias, E., and Smith, B. (2003). *Deaths: Preliminary data for 2001.* Hyattsville, MD: National Center for Health Statistics.

Arvanites, T. M. (2013). Segregation and African-American imprisonment rates for drug offenses. *Social Science Journal, 51,* 431–37.

Asante, M. K. (2003). *Afrocentricity: The theory of social change.* Chicago: African American Images.

Ascher, M., and Ascher, R. (1997). Ethnomathematics. In A. Powell and M. Frankenstein (Eds.), *Ethnomathematics, challenging Eurocentrism in mathematics education* (pp. 25–50). Albany: State University of New York Press.

Bachir, D., S. (2018). Négritude. In *The Stanford Encyclopedia of Philosophy* (Summer 2018 Edition), Edward N. Zalta (ed.). https://plato.stanford.edu/archives/ sum2018/entries/negritude.

Balfanz, R., Spiridakis, K., Neild, R., and Legters, N. (2003). *High poverty secondary schools and the juvenile justice system: How neither helps the other and how that could change* (Paper presentation). School to Prison Pipeline Conference, Harvard Civil Rights Project, Cambridge, MA. Retrieved from http://www.csos.jhu.edu/ crespar/techReports/Report70.pdf.

Balko, R. (2020, June). There's overwhelming evidence that the criminal justice system is racist. Here's the proof. *Washington Post.* Retrieved from https://www. washingtonpost.com/graphics/2020/opinions/systemic-racism-police-evidence -criminal-justice-system/.

Bandura, A. (1997). *Self-efficacy: The exercise of control.* New York: Freeman.

Banks, J. (2009). *The Routledge international companion to multicultural education.* New York: Routledge.

Banks, J., and Banks, C. (Eds.). (2004). *Handbook of research in multicultural education* (2nd ed.). San Francisco: Jossey-Bass.

Bascom, W. R. (1969). *The Yoruba of southwestern Nigeria.* New York: Holt, Rinehart and Winston.

Bauer, S. (2020, February). 5 ways prisoners were used for profit throughout U.S. history. *PBS News Hour.* Retrieved from https://www.pbs.org/newshour/arts/5-ways -prisoners-were-used-for-profit-throughout-u-s-history.

Bean, T., and Harper, H. (2007). Reading men differently: Alternative portrayals of masculinity in contemporary young adult fiction. *Reading Psychology, 28,* 1–30.

Bendroth, L., and Brereton, V. L. (2003). Women and twentieth-century Protestantism. *Sociology of Religion, 64*(2), 273–74.

Benner, M., Brown, C., and Jeffery, A. (2019, August). *Elevating student voice in education.* Retrieved from https://www.americanprogress.org/issues/education-k -12/reports/2019/08/14/473197/elevating-student-voice-education/.

Betty, B. (2015). *Assumicide: Assumptions that kill learning.* Retrieved from http://static1.1.sqspcdn.com/static/f/659196/14418982/1317415612163/ Assumicide+Feb06.pdf?token=ofR8zNt5B4kKQtnO0%2FgnQ96R3%2FU%3D.

Blalock, H. M. (1967). *Toward a theory of minority-group relations*. New York: Wiley.

Blesser, A. (2014, June). *A Black college student has the same chances of getting a job as a White high school dropout*. Think Progress. Retrieved from http://thinkprogress.org/education/2014/06/25/3452887/education-race-gap/.

Bligh, R. (2013, May). Poverty and student achievement: Are we comparing the wrong groups? *Washington Post*.

Blinder, R. (2015, September). Elisabeth Hasselbeck suggests the Black Lives Matter movement is a hate group. *New York Daily News*. Retrieved from http://www.nydailynews.com/news/national/elisabeth-hasselbeck-Black-lives-matter-hate-group-article-1.2344132.

Blocker, D., Romocki, L., Thomas, K., Jones, B., Jackson, E., Reid, L., and Campbell, M. (2006, August). Knowledge, beliefs, and barriers associated with prostate cancer prevention and screening behaviors among African-American men. *Journal of the National Medical Association, 98*(8), 1286–95.

Bonczar, T. P. (2003). *Prevalence of imprisonment in the U.S. population, 1974–2001*. Washington, DC: US Department of Justice.

Borrelli, L. (2021, June). HBCUS and how to support them. Best Value Schools. Retrieved at: https://www.bestvalueschools.com/faq/impact-of-hbcus/.

Botelho, G., Jorgensen, S., and Netto, J. (2016, January). *The water crisis in Flint, Michigan, draws federal investigation*. CNN. Retrieved from http://www.cnn.com/2016/01/05/health/flint-Michigan-water-investigation/.

Bourdieu, P. (1986). The forms of capital. In J. G. Richardson (Ed.), *Handbook of theory and research for the sociology of education* (pp. 241–58). New York: Greenwood.

Bourdieu, P., and Passeron, J. C. (1979). *The inheritors: French students and their relations to culture*. Chicago: University of Chicago Press.

Boykin, A. W. (1983). On academic task performance and Afro-American children. In J. T. Spence (Ed.), *Achievement and achievement motives* (pp. 324–71). Boston: W. H. Freeman.

Brandt, A. M. (1978). Racism and research: The case of the Tuskegee Syphilis Study. *Hastings Center Report, 8*(6), 21–29.

Bridge Builders. (2022). Understanding African American male college graduation rates in 2020. Bridge builders foundation. Retrieved at: https://www.bridgebuildersla.org/african-american-male-college-graduation-rates-2020/.

Browder, A. T. (1992). *Nile valley contributions to civilization: Exploding the myths (Vol. 1)*. Washington, DC: Institute of Karmic Guidance.

Brown, B. B. (2004). Adolescents' relationships with peers. In R. M. Lerner and L. Steinberg (Eds.), *Handbook of adolescent psychology* (2nd ed., pp. 363–94). Hoboken, NJ: Wiley.

Brown, J., & Doolittle, J. (2008). A cultural, linguistic, and ecological framework for response to intervention with English language learners. *Teaching Exceptional Children, 40*(5), 66–72.

Bryant, W. W. (2011). Internalized racism's association with African American male youth's propensity for violence. *Journal of Black Studies, 42*(4), 690–707. https://doi.org/10.1177/0021934710393243.

Buchholz, K. (2021, February). *Black incarceration rates are dropping in the U.S.* Statista. Retrieved from https://www.statista.com/chart/18376/us-incarceration-rates-by-sex-and-race-ethnic-origin/.

Bunn, C. (2022, March). Report: Black people are still killed by police at a higher rate than other groups. NBC News. Retrieved at: https://www.nbcnews.com/news/nbcblk/report-black-people-are-still-killed-police-higher-rate-groups-rcna17169.

Burris, B. (2013). *Student suspended for Pop-Tart gun.* National Institute on the Education of At-Risk Students. Retrieved from http://www2.ed.gov/pubs/ToolsforSchools/append_b.html.

Campanella, T. J. (2017, July). Robert Moses and his racist parkway, explained. BloombergCityLab. Retrieved from https://www.bloomberg.com/news/articles/2017-07-09/robert-moses-and-his-racist-parkway-explained.

Cartwright, A. (1858). The Caucasians and the Africans. *DeBow's Review, 25,* 51.

CBS News. (2014). Black students more likely to be suspended—even in preschool. Retrieved from http://www.cbsnews.com/news/education-department-Black-preschoolers-more-likely-to-be-suspended/.

Chandler, D. L. (2014, August). *Ferguson: Straight facts on #MikeBrown shooting case.* News One: For Black America. Retrieved from http://newsone.com/3047840/mike-brown-shooting-facts/.

Chapel, E. (2014, June). Black male depression: Therapist shares insight to reasons and warning signs. *Indianapolis Recorder.* Retrieved from http://www.indianapolisrecorder.com/health/article_3499c65a-ecb7-11e3-9bb1-0019bb2963f4.htmlr.

Cleveland, P. C. (2011). *Teaching boys who struggle in school.* Alexandria, VA: ASCD.

Connell, R. W. (1995). *Masculinities.* Cambridge: Polity Press.

Connell, R. W. (1996). Teaching boys: New research on masculinity, and gender strategies for schools. *Teachers College Record, 98*(2), 206–35.

Connell, R. W. (2000). *The men and the boys.* St. Leonards, NSW: Allen and Unwin.

Connell, R. W. (2002). *Gender.* Cambridge: Polity Press.

Connell, R. W. (2005). *Masculinities* (2nd ed.). Cambridge: Polity Press.

Cook, B. (2012). *By the numbers: More Black men in prison than in college? Think again.* American Council on Education. Retrieved from http://www.acenet.edu/the-presidency/columns-and-features/Pages/By-the-Numbers-More-Black-Men-in-Prison-Than-in-College-Think-Again-.aspx.

Corkett, J., Hatt, B., and Benevides, T. (2011). Student and teacher self-efficacy and the connection to reading and writing. *Canadian Journal of Education, 34*(1), 65–98. Retrieved from http://ezproxy.msu.edu/login?url=http://search.proquest.com/docview/871222504?accountid=12598.

Critical Resistance. (2015, June). *The prison industrial complex.* Retrieved from https://criticalresistance.org/mission-vision/not-so-common-language/.

Crundwell, R. M., and Killu, K. (2010). Responding to a student's depression. *Interventions That Work, 68*(2), 46–51.

Davis, L. P., and Museus, S. D. (2019). What is deficit thinking? An analysis of conceptualizations of deficit thinking and implications for scholarly research. *Currents, 1*(1), 117–30. http://dx.doi.org/10.3998/currents.17387731.0001.110.

De La Casa, V. (1994). "Coolin": The psychological communication of African and Latino men. In D. J. Jones (Ed.), *African American males: A critical link in the African American family*. New Brunswick, NJ: Transaction.

DeGruy, J. (2005). *Post-traumatic slave syndrome: America's legacy of enduring injury and healing.* Baltimore, MD: Uptone Press.

Didley-Marling, C. (2015). The resilience of deficit thinking. *Journal of Teaching and Learning 10*(1), 1–12.

Douglass, F. (1852/2006). *What, to the slave, is the fourth of July?* New York: Dover.

Du Bois, W. E. B. (1903). *The soul of Black folks*. New York: Dover.

Dudley-Marling, C. (2015). The resilience of deficit thinking. *Journal of Teaching and Learning, 10*(1), 1–12.

Duffin, E. (2021). Jail incarceration rate of confined inmates in the United States in 2020, by race/Hispanic origin. Retrieved from https://www.statista.com/statistics /816699/local-jail-inmates-in-the-united-states-by-race/.

Dweck, D. (2013). *Changing mindsets, motivating students with Carol Dweck.* Webinar Education Week. Retrieved July 17, 2013, from edweek.org/media/2012 -02-16_changingmindsets.pdf.

Dyson, M. (2007). *Debating race with Michael Eric Dyson.* New York: Basic Civitas Books.

Effiong, U., Hogan, E., and Obasi, O. (2020, October). *Infant mortality among Black babies*. University of Michigan's School of Public Health. Retrieved from https:// sph.umich.edu/pursuit/2020posts/infant-mortality-among-black-babies.html.

Eichler, A. (2010, July). Rap isn't Black America's CNN. *The Atlantic.* Retrieved from https://www.theatlantic.com/culture/archive/2010/10/rap-isn-t-black-america -s-cnn/339862/.

Eitle, D., D'Alessio, J., and Stolzenberg, L. (2002). Racial threat and social control: A test of the political, economic and the threat of Black crime hypotheses. *Social Forces 81*(2), 557–76.

Elfman, L. (2019, October). *HBCUs produce more upwardly mobile graduates than PWIs*. Diverse Issues in Higher Education. Retrieved from https://diverseeducation.com/leadership-policy/article/15105512/ report-hbcus-produce-more-upwardly-mobile-graduates-than-pwis.

Englash, R. (2005). *African fractals: Modern computing and indigenous design.* New Brunswick, NJ: Rutgers University Press.

Equal Justice Initiative. (2017, September). *Black children five times more likely to be incarcerated than White youth to be incarcerated.* Retrieved from https://eji. org/news/Black-children-five-times-more-likely-than-whites-to-be-incarcerated/.

ETS. (Winter, 2012). Middle School Matters: Improving the Life Course of Black Boy. Policy Notes: News from the ETS Policy Information Center, 20(4), 1–12.

European Network Against Racism. (2014). *Invisible visible minority: Confronting Afrophobia and advancing equality for people of African descent and Black Europeans in Europe*. Brussels: European Network Against Racism.

Eyerman, R. (2001). *Cultural trauma: Slavery and the formation of African American Identity*. Cambridge: Cambridge University Press.

Fabelo, T., Thompson, M., Plotkin, M., Carmichael, D., Marchbanks, M., and Booteh, E. (2011). *Breaking schools' rules: A statewide study of how school discipline relates to students' success and juvenile justice involvement*. College Station, TX: Public Policy Research Institute, Texas A&M University.

Fanon, F. (1967). *Black skin, White masks*. Translated by Charles Markmann. New York: Grove.

Fantz, A., Almasy, S., and Shoichet, C. E. (2015, December). *Tamir Rice shooting: No charges for officers*. CNN.com. Retrieved from http://www.cnn.com/2015/12/28/us/tamir-rice-shooting/index.html.

Faqs.org. (2014). *Peer pressure*. Retrieved from http://www.faqs.org/health/topics/76/Peer-pressure.html.

Ferlazzo, L. (2012). *A fascinating study on what learning from mistakes does to the brain*. Larry Ferlazzo's Websites of the Day. Retrieved July 9, 2013, from http://larryferlazzo.edublogs.org/2012/02/18/fascinating-study-on-what-learning-from-mistakes-does-to-the-brain/.

Finley, T. (2015, October). HBCU alumni are thriving more than Black grads of other schools, study shows. *Huffington Post*. Retrieved from http://www.huffingtonpost.com/entry/hbcu-alumni-are-thriving-more-than-black-grads-of-other-schools-study-shows_us_56310c1be4b0631799107aaa.

Ford, C. L., Whetten, K. D., Hall, S. A., Kaufman, J. S., and Thrasher, A. D. (2007). Black sexuality, social construction, and research targeting "the down low." *Annals of Epidemiology, 17*(3), 209–16.

Franklin, C. (1985). The Black male urban barbershop as a sex-role socialization setting. *Sex Roles, 12*(9–10), 965–79.

Freud, S. (1939). *Moses and monotheism*. London: Hogarth Press.

Frosh, S., Phoenix, A., and Pattman, R. (2002). *Young masculinities: Understanding boys in contemporary society*. Basingstoke: Palgrave.

Galtung, J., and Höivik, T. (1971). Structural and direct violence: A note on operationalization. *Journal of Peace Research, 8*(1), 73–76.

Gates, A. (2019). *Faculty interactions with Black male students at HBCUs and community colleges as predictors of academic achievement in STEM* (Doctoral dissertation). University of Southern Mississippi. Retrieved from https://aquila.usm.edu/dissertations/1692.

George, N. (2014). Hip-hop's founding fathers speak the truth. In M. Forman and M. Neal (Eds.), *That's the joint! The hip-hop studies reader*. New York, London: Routledge.

Gersten, R., & Dimino, J. A. (2006). RTI (Response to Intervention): Rethinking special education for students with reading difficulties (yet again). *Reading Research Quarterly, 41*(1), 99–108. https://doi.org/10.1598/RRQ.41.1.5.

Grant, J., and Richardson, T. (1998). *The retention/promotion checklist*. Peterborough, NH: Crystal Springs Books.

Green, C. (2018). *Against criminalization and pathology: The making of a Black achieve praxis* (Doctoral dissertation). City University of New York. Retrieved from https://academicworks.cuny.edu/cgi/viewcontent.cgi?article=3981&context =gc_etds.

Green, R. L. (2009). *Expectations: How teacher expectations can increase student achievement and assist in closing the achievement gap*. Columbus, OH: McGraw-Hill.

Green, R. L. (2014). *Expect the most provide the best: How high expectations, outstanding instruction, & curricular innovations help ass students succeed*. New York: Scholastic Books.

Gutierrez, J. R. (2020, November). *Corporations' use of prison labor*. Berkeley Law. Retrieved from https://sites.law.berkeley.edu/sustainability-compliance/ corporations-use-of-prison-labor/.

Haefeli. L. (2020, February). *Term "at-risk youth" replaced with "at-promise youth" in California penal codes*. CBS Sacramento. Retrieved from https://sacramento. cbslocal.com/2020/02/13/at-risk-youth-replaced-with-at-promise-youth-california -penal-codes/.

Hankerson, S. H., Suite, D., and Bailey, R. K. (2015). Treatment disparities among African American men with depression: Implications for clinical practice. *Journal of Health Care Poor Underserved, 26*(1), 21–34. https://doi.org/10.1353/ hpu.2015.0012.

Hannor-Walker, T., Bohecker, L., Ricks, L., and Kitchens, S. (2020). Experiences of Black adolescents with depression in rural communities. *Professional Counselor, 10*(2), 285. https://doi.org/10.15241/thw.10.2.285.

Harkinson, J. (2014, August). 4 unarmed *Black men have been killed by police in the last month*. Motherjones.com. Retrieved from http://www.motherjones.com/ politics/2014/08/3-unarmed-Black-African-American-men-killed-police.

Harris, F., and Harper, S. R. (2008). Masculinities go to college: Understanding male identity socialization and gender role conflict. In J. Lester (Ed.), *Gendered perspectives in community colleges. New directions for community colleges* (pp. 25–35). San Francisco: Jossey-Bass.

Harris, M. D. (1992). Africentrism and curriculum: Concepts, issues, and prospects. *Journal of Negro Education, 61*, 301–16.

Harris-Perry, M. (2014, August). *The deaths of Black men in America*. MSNBC. Retrieved from https://www.msnbc.com/melissa-harris-perry/watch/ the-deaths-of-black-men-in-america-318795331819.

Harvard Civil Rights Project. (1999). Harvard civil rights project reports rise in school segregation. *Harvard Civil Rights Project, 10*(4). Retrieved from http:// www.civilrights.org/monitor/fall1999/art6p1.html.

Hattie, J. (2012). *Visible learning for teachers: Maximizing impact on learning*. New York: Routledge.

Head, J. (2005). *Black men and depression: Saving our lives, healing our families and friends*. New York: Harlem Moon Broadway Books.

Health, B. (2014, November). The racial gap in U.S. arrest rates: "Staggering dispar-ity." *USA Today*. Retrieved from http://www.usatoday.com/story/news/nation/2014/11/18/ferguson-Black-arrest-rates/19043207/.

Henderson-Hubbard, L. D. (2011). *Urban African-American single mothers using resiliency and racial socialization to influence academic success in their young sons* (Dissertation). Texas A&M University.

Henkeman, S. M. (2016, April). *How violence and racism are related and why it all matters*. The Conversation. Retrieved from https://theconversation.com/how-violence-and-racism-are-related-and-why-it-all-matters-65738.

Henrich, J., Heine, S. J., and Norenzayan, A. (2010). The weirdest people in the world? *Behavioral and Brain Sciences, 33*(2/3), 1–75.

Hicks, S. R. (2015). *A critical analysis of post-traumatic slave syndrome: A mul-tigenerational legacy of slavery* (Order No. 3712420). Available from ProQuest Dissertations and Theses A&I; ProQuest Dissertations & Theses Global. (1707689965). Retrieved from http://ezproxy.msu.edu.proxy2.cl.msu.edu/login?url=http://search.proquest.com.proxy2.cl.msu.edu/docview/1707689965?accountid=12598.

Hickson, M. E. (2002). What role does the race of professors have on the retention of students attending historically Black colleges and universities. *Education, 123*(1), 186–89.

Hoetetter, M., and Klein, S. (2021, January). *Understanding medical mistrust among Black Americans*. Commonwealth Fund. Retrieved from https://www.commonwealthfund.org/publications/newsletter-article/2021/jan/medical-mistrust-among-black-americans.

hooks, b. (2004). *We real cool: Black men and masculinity*. New York: Routledge.

Howard, T. (2008). Who really cares? The disenfranchisement of African American males in prek–12 schools: A critical race theory perspective. *Teachers College Record, 110*(5), 954–85.

Hunt, A., and Robles, D. J. (2018, June). Depression in Black boys begins earlier than you think. *Psychology Benefits Society*. Retrieved from https://psychologybenefits.org/2018/06/29/depression-in-black-boys-begins-earlier-than-you-think/.

Hyra, D. S., Squires, D. G., Renner, R. N., and Kirk, D. S. (2013). Metropolitan segregation and the subprime lending crisis. *Housing Policy Debate, 23*(1), 177–98. Available from https://www.researchgate.net/publication/259693593_Metropolitan_Segregation_and_the_Subprime_Lending_Crisis.

Inzlicht, M., Legault, L., and Teper, R. (2014). Exploring the mechanisms of self-control improvement. *Current Directions in Psychological Science, 23*(4), 302–7. https://doi.org/10.1177/0963721414534256.

Jackson, C., and Dempster, S. (2009, December). "I sat back on my computer . . . with a bottle of whisky next to me": Constructing "cool" masculinity through "effort-less" achievement in secondary and higher education. *Journal of Gender Studies, 18*(4), 341–56.

Jackson, Y. (2011). *Pedagogy of confidence: Inspiring high intellectual performance in an urban school*. New York: Teachers College Press.

Johnson, E. (2019). *Racial inequality, at college and in the workplace.* Inside Higher Ed. Retrieved from https://www.insidehighered.com/news/2019/10/18/racial-inequality-college-and-workplace.

Johnson, K. (2000, May 26). *The peer effect on academic achievement among public elementary students* (CDA Report No. 00-06). Washington, DC: Heritage Center for Data Analysis, Heritage Foundations.

Jones, C. P. (2000). Levels of racism: A theoretic framework and a gardener's tale. *American Journal of Public Health, 90*(8), 1212–15. https://doi.org/10.2105/AJPH.90.8.1212.

Jones, J. (2022, February). 3 ex-officers found guilty of violating George Floyd's civil rights in federal trial. MSNBC. Retrieved at: https://www.msnbc.com/the-reidout/reidout-blog/george-floyd-verdict-rcna17562.

Jones, V. (2007, January). *Van Jones at the National Conference for Media Reform.* Memphis: NCMR and Free Press. Uploaded January 6, 2007. http://www.youtube.com/watch?v=n2z6n000-2Y.

Jung, C. G. (1966). *The spirit in man, art, and literature.* New York: Pantheon.

Kahn, J. (2004). How a drug becomes ethnic. *Yale Journal of Health Policy, Law, and Ethics, 4*(1), 1–46.

Kaplan, V., and Rose, B. (1999). *Treatment of hypertension in Blacks.* Wolters Kluwer. Retrieved January 31 from http://www.uptodate.com/contents/treatment-of-hypertension-in-Blacks?source=search_result&search=Thiazide+diuretics&selectedTitle=20~150.

Katznelson, I. (2005). *When affirmative action was White: An untold history of racial inequality in twentieth-century America.* New York: Norton.

Kauffman, P Bradbury, D. & Owings, J. (1992). *National Education Longitudinal Study of 1988: Characteristics of at-risk students in NELS:88.*

Kazemi, S, Ashraf, H. Motallebzadeh K. & Zeraatpishe, M. (2020) Development and validation of a null curriculum questionnaire focusing on 21st century skills using the Rasch model. *Cogent Education, 7*(1), 1–17. DOI: 10.1080/2331186X.2020.1736849.

King, J. L. (2004). *On the down-low.* New York: Broadway.

King, M. J. (2013). *Realizing a dream: 50 years after the march on Washington.* New York State University. Retrieved from https://www.nyu.edu/washington-dc/nyu-washington--dc-events/realizing-a-dream.html.

King, R. D., and Wheelock, D. (2007). Group threat and social control: Race, perceptions of minorities and the desire to punish. *Social Forces 85*(3), 1255–80.

Klisz-Hulbert, R. (2020, *July). African American teens face mental health crisis but are less likely than whites to get treatment.* The Conversation. Retrieved from https://theconversation.com/african-american-teens-face-mental-health-crisis-but-are-less-likely-than-whites-to-get-treatment-140697.

Kuebler, M., and Rugh, J. (2013). New evidence on racial and ethnic disparities in homeownership in the United States from 2001 to 2010. *Social Science Research,* 1357–74.

Kunjufu, J. (2004). *Countering the conspiracy to destroy Black boys.* Chicago: African American Images.

Ladson-Billings, G. (2017). The (R)Evolution will not be standardized: Teacher education, Hip Hop pedagogy, and culturally relevant pedagogy 2.0. In D. Paris and H. S. Alim (Eds.), *Culturally sustaining pedagogies: Teaching and learning for justice in a changing world* (pp. 141–56). New York: Teachers College Press.

Ladson-Billings, G., and Tate, W. F., IV. (1995). Toward a critical race theory of education. *Teachers College Record, 97*(1), 47–68.

Latzer, B. (2016). *The rise and fall of violent crime in America.* New York: NY Encounter Books.

Laube, C., Lorenz, R., & van den Bos, W. (2020). Pubertal testosterone correlates with adolescent impatience and dorsal striatal activity. *Developmental cognitive neuroscience, 42*, 100749. https://doi.org/10.1016/j.dcn.2019.100749.

Lawnix. (2014). *Plessy v. Ferguson—Case Brief Summary.* Retrieved from http://www.lawnix.com/cases/plessy-ferguson.html.

Lee, M. (2015, June). Yes, U.S. locks people up at a higher rate than any other country. *Washington Post.* Retrieved from https://www.washingtonpost.com/news/fact-checker/wp/2015/07/07/yes-u-s-locks-people-up-at-a-higher-rate-than-any-other-country/.

Lemelle, A., Harrington, C., and LeBlanc, A. (Eds.). (2000). *Readings in the sociology of AIDS.* Upper Saddle River, NJ: Prentice Hall.

Levintova, H., Raja, T., Simones, I., and Vicens, A. (2014, August). *Ferguson is 60 percent Black: Virtually all the cops are white.* Mother Jones. Retrieved from http://www.motherjones.com/politics/2014/08/10-insane-numbers-ferguson-killing.

Lindsey, M. A., Sheftall, A. H., Xiao, Y., and Sean, J. (2019). Trends of suicidal behaviors among high school students in the United States: 1991–2017. *Journal of the Academy of Pediatrics, 144*(5), 1–18.

Literacy Mid-South. (2016, March). *The relationship between incarceration and low literacy.* Retrieved from https://www.literacymidsouth.org/news/the-relationship-between-incarceration-and-low-literacy/.

Lombardo, G. (2015). *Sherriff's African American advisory committee board meeting.* Las Vegas: Nevada Partners.

Losen, D., and Skiba, R. (2010). *Suspended education: Urban middle school in crisis.* Los Angeles: University of California Los Angeles, Civil Rights Project.

Majors, R., and Billson, J. M. (1992). *Cool pose: The dilemmas of Black manhood in America.* New York: Lexington Books.

Malone, B. (2003). Chief Rocka. *Source Magazine: The Magazine of Hip-Hop Music, Culture, Politics (fifteenth anniversary jumpoff), 167*, 130–33.

Mandelbrot, B. (1977). *Fractals: Form, chance and dimension.* London: Freeman.

Marshall, K. (2009). A how-to plan for widening the gap. *Phi Delta Kappan 90*(9), 650–55.

McDougal, S. I., II. (2007). *An Afrocentric analysis of teacher/student style congruency and high school Black male achievement levels.* Order No. 3293237, Temple University. ProQuest Dissertations and Theses, 342. Retrieved from http://ezproxy.msu.edu/login?url=http://search.proquest.com/docview/304818503?accountid=12598. (304818503).

McGee, E. O., and Bentley, L. C. (2017). The equity ethic: Black and Latinx college students reengineering their STEM careers toward justice. *American Journal of Education, 124*(1), 1–36. https://doi.org/10.1086/693954.

Mcintosh, K., Davis, J., Garraway, R. L., and Burt, J. M. (2018). Every student succeeds (except for Black males) act. *Teachers College Record, 120*(13), 1–20.

McKenry, P., Everett, J., Ramseur, H., and Carter, C. (1989). Research on Black adolescents: A legacy of cultural bias. *Journal of Adolescent Research, 4*(2), 254–64.

Michigan Department of Education. (2013). African-American male student voice: Report on Ingham County focus groups.

Michigan Department of Education Achievement Gap. (2021). *The positive phone call home intervention: Evidence-based implementation brief.* Retrieved from https://www.michigan.gov/documents/mde/AG_Positive_Calls_Home_415756_7.pdf.

Milner, H. R., and Howard, T. C. (2004). Black teachers, black students, black communities, and brown: Perspectives and insights from experts. *Journal of Negro Education, 73*(3), 285–97. Retrieved from http://ezproxy.msu.edu.proxy1.cl.msu.edu/login.

Morisano, D. (2010). Setting, elaborating, and reflecting on personal goals improves academic performance. *Journal of Applied Psychology, 95*(2), 255–64.

Murphy, J. (2010). *Understanding and closing achievement gaps.* Thousand Oaks, CA: Corwin.

Nafiu, O. O., Mpody, C., Kim S. S., Uffman J. C., and Tobias, J. D. (2020). Race, postoperative complications, and death in apparently healthy children. *Journal of the American Academy of Pediatrics, 146*(2). https://doi.org/10.1542/peds.2019-4113. Epub 2020 July 20. PMID: 32690804.

Naphan-Kingery, D. E., Miles, M., Brockman, A., McKane, R., Botchway, P., and McGee, E. (2019). Investigation of an equity ethic in engineering and computing doctoral students. *Journal of Engineering Education, 108*, 337–54. https://doi.org/10.1002/jee.20284.

National Center for Education Statistics. (2020). *Historically Black colleges and universities.* Retrieved from https://nces.ed.gov/fastfacts/display.asp?id=667.

National Institute on the Education of At-Risk Students. (1988). *Appendix B.* Retrieved from http://www2.ed.gov/pubs/ToolsforSchools/append_b.html.

Neal, L., et al. (2003). The effects of African American movement styles on teachers' perceptions and reactions. *Journal of Special Education, 37*(1), 49–57.

Neal, M. A. (2002). *Soul babies: Black popular culture and the post-soul aesthetic.* New York: Routledge.

Neito, S. (2004). *Affirming diversity: The sociopolitical context of multicultural education* (4th ed.). Boston: Pearson.

Nicholson, C. K. (1968). *Anthropology and education.* Columbus, OH: Chalres E. Merrill Publishing Co.

Nielsen, C. (2013). Frantz Fanon and the nägritude movement: How strategic essentialism subverts Manichean binaries. *Callaloo, 36*(2), 342–52. Retrieved at http://www.jstor.org/stable/24264913.

North Carolina Digital History. (2010). *A bill to prevent all persons from teaching slaves to read or write, the use of figures excepted (1830).* Legislative Papers, 1830–31, Session of the General Assembly. Retrieved from http://www.learnnc.org /lp/editions/nchist-newnation/4384.

North Carolina General Assembly. (1830). *A bill to prevent all persons from teaching slaves to read or write, the use of figures excepted (1830).* Legislative Papers, 1830–31, Session of the General Assembly. Retrieved from http://www.learnnc.org /lp/editions/nchist-newnation/4384.

Ntinu, V. I. W. (2019). *"It's the way the world is set up, to believe Africans are less": The significance of Afrophobia in the way second generation Afro-citizens navigate their Western citizenship—A comparative analysis between the Netherlands and Greece* (Master's thesis). University of Van Amsterdam, Netherlands.

Nunes, S., and Loos-Sant'Ana, H. (2015). Self-concept, self-esteem and self-efficacy: The role of self-beliefs in the coping process of socially vulnerable adolescents. *Journal of Latino/Latin American Studies, 7*(1), 33–44.

Office for Civil Rights. (2015). *Civil rights data center.* Ed.gov. Retrieved from http://ocrdata.ed.gov/.

Office of Equal Opportunity and Diversity. (2015). *A brief history of affirmative action.* Retrieved June 22, 2022, from https://www.oeod.uci.edu/policies/aa_history.php.

Office of the High Commissioner. (1965). *International convention on the elimination of all forms of racial discrimination, resolution 2106 (XX).* Office of the High Commissioner for Human Rights. Retrieved from https://www.ohchr.org/en/professionalinterest/pages/cerd.aspx.

Orfield, G. & Yun, J. T. (1999). *Resegregation in American schools. The civil rights project.* Cambridge, MA: Harvard University.

Palazzolo, J. (2013). Racial gaps in men's sentencing. *Wall Street Journal.* Retrieved from http://www.wsj.com/articles/SB100014241278873244320045783044637898 58002#printMode.

Pediatrics, P. (2021, April). *Teen depression during COVID-19 pandemic: What to look for.* Retrieved from https://www.scripps.org/news_items/5319-teen-depression -during-covid-19-pandemic-what-to-look-for.

Pelaez, V. (2008). *The prison industry in the United States: Big business or a new form of slavery?* Retrieved October 3, 2010, from http://www.globalresearch.ca/index.php?context=va&aid=8289.

Perry, A. M., and Harshbarger, D. (2019, October). *America's formerly redlined neighborhoods have changed, and so must solutions to rectify them.* Brookings. Retrieved from https://www.brookings.edu/research/americas-formerly-redlines -areas-changed-so-must-solutions/.

Perry, T., Steele, C., and Hilliard, A., III. (2003). *Young gifted and Black: Promoting high achievement among African-American students.* New York: Beacon Press.

Pescale, R., and Primavera, L. (2019, April). Male and female brains: Are they wired differently? *Psychology Today.* Retrieved from https://www.psychologytoday.com/us/blog/so-happy-together/201904/male-and-female-brains.

Pollack, William S. (1998). *Real boys: Rescuing our sons from the myths of boyhood.* New York: Henry Holt and company.

Pope, J. (2009, May 11). *Obama's education budget cuts $85 mil from HBCUs.* Black America Web. Retrieved from http://hbcuconnect.com/content/139887/obama-s-education-budget-cuts-85-mil-from-hbcus.

Portes, A. (1998). Social capital: Its origins and applications in modern sociology. *Annual Review of Sociology, 24,* 1–24.

Prince, Z., and Edney, T. (2015). The success of HBCU alumni surpasses other grads. *Jacksonville Free Press.*

Princeton University Press. (2015). *Nihilism.* Princeton, NJ: Princeton University. Retrieved from press.princeton.edu/chapters/s9593.pdf.

Quillian, L., and Devah, P. (2001). Black neighbors, higher crime? The role of racial stereotypes in evaluations of neighborhood crime. *American Journal of Sociology, 107*(3), 717–67.

Rampey, B., Finnegan, R., Goodman, M., Mohadjer, L., Krenzke, T., Hogan, J., Provasnik, S., and Xie, H. (2016). *Skills of U.S. unemployed, young, and older adults in sharper focus: Results from the program for the international assessment of adult competencies (PIAAC) 2012/2014: First look.* Washington, DC: US Department of Education, Institute of Education Sciences.

Ransaw, T. (2012). *A father's hands: African American fathering involvement and the educational outcomes of their children* (Doctoral dissertation). University of Nevada, Las Vegas. ProQuest Dissertations and Theses Global. http://dx.doi.org/10.34917/4332593.

Ransaw, T. (2013). *The art of being cool: The pursuit of Black masculinity.* Chicago: African American Images.

Ransaw, T. (2014). The good father: African American fathers who positively influence the educational outcomes of their children. *Spectrum: A Journal on Black Men, 2*(2), 1–26.

Ransaw, T., and Green, R. L. (2016). Black males, peer pressure and high expectations. In T. Ransaw and R. Majors (Eds.), *Closing achievement gaps for African American males.* East Lansing, MI: Michigan State University Press.

Ransaw, T., and Majors, R. (Eds.). (2016). *Closing achievement gaps for African American males.* East Lansing, MI: Michigan State University Press.

Ravich, D. (2000). *Left-back.* New York: Simon & Schuster.

Reilly, R. (2014, November). Ferguson officer Darren Wilson was not indicted in the Michael Brown shooting. *Huffington Post.* Retrieved from http://www.huffingtonpost.com/2014/11/24/michael-brown-grand-jury_n_6159070.html.

Reiland, R. (2009). Van's line. *New Spectator.* Retrieved October 4, 2010, from http://www.thenewspectator.org/archives/2009/09/17/vans-line.

Riccio, C. A., Hewitt, L. L., & Blake, J. J. (2011). Relation of measures of executive function to aggressive behavior in children. *Applied neuropsychology, 18*(1), 1–10. https://doi.org/10.1080/09084282.2010.525143.

Roberts, S. O., Bareket-Shavit, C., Dollins, F. A., Goldie, P. D., and Mortenson, E. (2020). Racial inequality in psychological research: Trends of the past and recommendations for the future. *Perspectives on Psychological Science, 15*(6), 1295–1309. https://doi.org/10.1177/1745691620927709.

Roebuck, J. B., and Murty, K. B. (1993). *Historically Black colleges and universities: Their place in American higher education.* Westport, CT: Bergin and Garvey.

Schippers, M. C., Scheepers, A. W. A., and Peterson, J. B. (2015). A scalable goal -setting intervention closes both the gender and ethnic minority achievement gap. *Palgrave Communications, 14*, 1–12.

Schmidt, W. H. (2015, September). *Failed mission: How schools worsen inequality.* New York: New York Teachers College Press.

Seiden, R. (1970). We're driving young Black men to suicide. *Psychology Today, 4*, 24–28.

Serrano, A. (2018, February). *Juvenile injustice: Racial disparities in incarceration start early.* Color Lines. Retrieved from https://www.colorlines.com/articles/juvenile-injustice-racial-disparities-incarceration-start-early.

Shanahan, C., Shanahan, T., and Misischia, C. (2011). Analysis of expert readers in three disciplines: History, mathematics, and chemistry. *Journal of Literacy Research, 43*(4), 393–429. https://doi.org/10.1177/1086296X11424071.

Shapiro, A. (Producer). (2017, May). *"The color of law" details how U.S. housing policies created segregation* (Audio podcast). NPR. https://www.npr.org/2017/05/17/528822128/the-color-of-law-details-how-u-s-housing-policies-created-segregation.

Shapiro, J. P., and Gross, S. J. (2013). *Ethical educational leadership in turbulent times: (Re)solving moral dilemmas* (2nd ed.). New York: Routledge. https://doi.org/10.4324/9780203809310.

Shindler, J. (2009). *Transformative classroom management: Positive strategies to engage all students and promote a psychology of success.* San Francisco: Jossey-Bass.

Slaughter-Defoe, D. T., and Rubin, H. (2001). A longitudinal case study of Head Start eligible children: Implications for urban education. *Educational Psychologist, 36*(1), 31–44.

Smith, B. (1965). *They closed their schools.* Chapel Hill: University of North Carolina Press.

Smitherman, G. (1998). *Talkin that talk.* New York: Routledge.

Smollin, M. (2010). *Zero tolerance almost doubles school suspensions.* Take Part: Inspiration to Action. Retrieved October 30, 2010, from http://www.takepart.com/news/2010/09/22/zero-tolerancealmost-doubles-school-suspensions.

Stafford, A., Freeman, J. P., & Vianden, J. (2010). Helping college men transcend the "boy problem": A call to union and activities professionals. *The Bulletin, 79*(3), 28–35.

Statista. (2021). Jail incarceration rate of confined inmates in the United States in 2019, by race/Hispanic origin. Retrieved at https://www.statista.com/statistics/816699/local-jail-inmates-in-the-united-states-by-race/.

Steinberg, L. (1993). *Adolescence* (3rd ed.). New York: McGraw-Hill.

Sue, D. W., Capodilupo, C. M., Torino, G. C., Bucceri, J. M., Holder, A. M. B., Nadal, K. L., and Esquilin, M. (2007). Racial microaggressions in everyday life: Implications for clinical practice. *American Psychologist, 62*(4), 271–86. https://doi.org/10.1037/0003-066X.62.4.271.

Sullivan, A., and Sheffrin, S. A. (2003). *Economics: Principles in action.* Upper Saddle River, NJ: Pearson Prentice Hall.

Superintendent's Educational Opportunity Advisory Council. (2013, February). *Overrepresentation by gender, race/ethnicity, or disability in discipline-related actions and/or special education placement.* Las Vegas, NV: Clark County School District.

Thomas, A. E., and Green, R. L. (2001). Historical Black colleges and universities: An irreplaceable national treasure. In Cynthia L. Jackson, *African American education: A references handbook* (pp. 245–65). Santa Barbara, CA: ABC-CLIO.

Trivani Foundation. (2009). *Trivani foundation newsletter: Family literacy centers.* Retrieved October 2, 2010, from http://www.trivanifoundation.org/news/marnewsletter09.pdf.

Tsai, T, & Scommegna, P. (2012). The U.S. has the world's highest incarceration rate. *Population Reference Bureau.* Retrieved from https://www.prb.org/resources/u-s-has-worlds-highest-incarceration-rate/.

United Nations. (2013). *Resolution 68/237. Proclamation of the international decade for people of African descent.* Retrieved from http://www.un.org/en/ga/search/view_doc.asp?symbol=A/RES/68/237.

US Commission on Civil Rights. (2019). *Beyond suspensions.* Retrieved from https://www.usccr.gov/pubs/2019/07-23-Beyond-Suspensions.pdf.

US Const. sec. 1, amend. XII. Retrieved from https://www.law.cornell.edu/constitution/amendmentxiii.

US Department of Education. (2009). *White House initiative on historically Black colleges and universities.* Retrieved November 3, 2009, from http://www.ed.gov/about/inits/list/whhbcu/edlite-index.html.

US Department of Education. (2018, November). *A leak in the STEM.* Retrieved from https://www2.ed.gov/datastory/stem/algebra/index.html.

US Department of Education, Office for Civil Rights. (2001). *Elementary and secondary school survey: National and state projections.* Washington, DC: US Government Printing Office.

US Department of Health and Human Services. (2021). *Asthma and African Americans.* Retrieved from https://minorityhealth.hhs.gov/omh/browse.aspx?lvl=4&lvlid=15.

US Department of Justice. (2010, June). *Prison inmates at midyear 2009—statistical tables.* Washington, DC: Bureau of Justice Statistics.

US Department of Labor. (2021). *History of executive order 11246.* Office of Federal Contract Compliance Programs. Retrieved from https://www.dol.gov/agencies/ofccp/about/executive-order-11246-history.

Van Breda, A. D. (2001). *Resilience theory: A literature review.* Pretoria, South Africa: South African Military Health Service. Retrieved from http://www.vanbreda.org/adrian/resilience.htm.

van Gennep, A. (1960). *The rites of passage.* Translated by M. B. Vizedom and G. L. Caffee. Chicago: University of Chicago Press.

Valencia, R. (Ed.). (1997). *The evolution of deficit thinking: Educational thought and practice.* Briston, PA: Falmer Press.

Wald, J., and Losen, D. (2003). Defining and redirecting a school-to-prison pipeline. In J. Wald and D. Losen (Eds.), *Deconstructing the school-to-prison pipeline: New directions for youth development (Number 99).* San Francisco: Jossey-Bass.

Walker, M. (2007, May). Study: HBCU graduates earn less than Black graduates of traditionally White institutions. *Diverse Issues in Higher Education.* Retrieved at: https://www.diverseeducation.com/institutions/hbcus/article/15083465/study-hbcu-graduates-earn-less-than-black-graduates-of-traditionally-white-institutions.

Wedgwood, N. (2009). Connell's theory of masculinity—its origins and influences on the study of gender. *Journal of Gender Studies, 18*(4), 329–39.

Welch, K. (2007). Black criminal stereotypes and racial profiling. *Journal of Contemporary Criminal Justice, 23*(3), 276–88.

Wenglinsky, H. (1999). *Historically Black colleges and universities: Their aspirations and accomplishments.* Princeton, NJ: Educational Testing Service.

Wesling, F. C. (1991). *The Isis papers: The keys to the colors.* Chicago: Third World Press.

Whitfield, S. (1991). *A death in the delta: The story of Emmett Till.* Baltimore, MD: Johns Hopkins University Press.

Wieviorka, M. (2013). Social conflict. *Criminal Sociology Review, 61*(5–6), 696–713.

Wildener, A. (2020, September). *Who has the most success preparing Black students for careers in science? Historically Black Colleges and Universities.* Chemical & Enginerring News. Retrieved from https://cen.acs.org/education/success-preparing-Black-students-careers/98/i34.

Willis, H. A., Sosoo, E. E., Bernard, D. L., Neal, A., and Neblett, E. W. (2021). The associations between internalized racism, racial identity, and psychological distress. *Emerging Adulthood.* https://doi.org/10.1177/21676968211005598.

Wilson, B. D. M., Harper, G. W., Hidalgo, M. A., Jamil, O. B., Torres, R. S., Isabel Fernandez, M., and Adolescent Medicine Trials Network for HIV/AIDS Interventions. (2010). Negotiating dominant masculinity ideology: Strategies used by gay, bisexual and questioning male adolescents. *American Journal of Community Psychology, 45*(1), 169–85. https://doi.org/10.1007/s10464-009-9291-3.

Woodson, C. (1933/1990). *The mis-education of the negro.* Trenton, NJ: Africa World Press.

Wyman, P. A., Cowen, E. L., Work, W. C., and Kerley, J. H. (1993). The role of children's future expectations in self-system functioning and adjustment to life-stress. *Development and Psychopathology, 5*, 649–61.

Yeager, D. S., Purdie-Vaughns, V., Garcia, J., Apfel, N., Brzustoski, P., Master, A., Hessert, W. T., Williams, M. E., and Cohen, G. L. (2014). Breaking the cycle of mistrust: Wise interventions to provide critical feedback across the racial divide. *Journal of Experimental Psychology, 143*(2), 804–24.

Yosso, T. (2005). Whose culture has capital? A critical race theory discussion of community cultural wealth. *Race, Ethnicity and Education, 8*(1), 69–91.

Zamosky, L. (2011, March). *How boys and girls learn differently: Do your son's fidgeting and wriggling mean he's checked out at school? Don't worry—he's perfectly normal.* WebMD. Retrieved from http://www.webmd.com/parenting/features/how-boys-and-girls-learn-differently.

Zill, N., and Wilcox, W. B. (2019, November). *The Black White divide in suspensions: What is the role of family?* Institute for Family Studies. Retrieved from https://ifstudies.org/blog/the-black-white-divide-in-suspensions-what-is-the-role-of-family.

Index

teacher survey in, 83–86; RTI and
MTSS implementation survey
in, 86–88; teacher and school
abandonment in, 57
Tuskegee Experiment (Study of
Untreated Syphilis in the Male
Negro), 36

United Nations, discrimination
definition of, 41

Washington, Booker T., 59
Watzlawick, P., 68
WEIRD. *See* Western, educated,
industrialized, rich, and
Democratic societies
Welch, O. M., 70
Western, educated, industrialized,
rich, and Democratic societies
(WEIRD), 26

Wharton, Clifton, 60
*What, to the Slave, Is the Fourth of
July?* (Douglass, F.), 19
White Racial Identity Attitude Scale
(WRIAS), 61
Whitmore, R. W., 71
Willis, H. A., 35
Wilson, Darren, M. Brown incident
involving, 3
Woodson, Carter G., 3, 17, 59
WRIAS. *See* White Racial Identity
Attitude Scale
Wright, Daunte, 4

Yeager, D. S., 50

zero-tolerance policies, 14, 19,
22, 48, 61
Zimmerman, George, 62

About the Author

Theodore S. Ransaw is an equity and literacy outreach specialist for the Office of K–12 Outreach in the College of Education, core faculty member of African and African American studies, and affiliated faculty, Center for Gender in Global Context at Michigan State University. He received his PhD in curriculum and instruction from the University of Nevada, Las Vegas, focusing on multicultural and international education. Dr. Ransaw is the former Michigan achievement gap specialist for males of color, a former director of the Lion's Den Black male mentorship program for at-risk youth, a certified education coach, and a cognitive-behavioral therapist practitioner. He has three interrelated research areas: parental involvement, reading identity, and student achievement. Dr. Ransaw has several academic journal publications and is a coeditor of *The International Handbook of Black Community Mental Health*, an author and senior coeditor of *The Handbook of Research on Black Males*, senior editor for the book series *International Race and Education* published by Michigan State University Press, and the author of *The Art of Being Cool: The Pursuit of Black Masculinity.*

Work Email: ransawth@msu.edu
Email: instituteofaamales@gmail.com
Website: https://www.instituteofafricanamericanmales.com/
Facebook: https://www.facebook.com/IAAM01
Twitter: https://twitter.com/Transaw
LinkedIn: https://www.linkedin.com/in/theodore-ransaw-23773b15/
YouTube Channel:
https://www.youtube.com/channel/UCw5FCrRtpNfaQTH26M9KMDg